CLOSE ENCOUNTERS
OF THE THIRD KIND

CLOSE ENCOUNTERS
OF THE THIRD KIND

THE ULTIMATE VISUAL HISTORY

BY **MICHAEL KLASTORIN**
FOREWORD BY **STEVEN SPIELBERG**

TITAN BOOKS

London

CONTENTS

FOREWORD 6

INTRODUCTION 8

PART ONE

THEY CAME FROM BEYOND 12

LOOKING TO THE SKIES 14

SPIELBERG'S FIRST DRAFT 20

TWO ROADS DIVERGED 24

THE NEXT STEP 26

DESIGNING A BIGGER "BOX" 28

THE SECOND DRAFT 30

GOING "GREEN" 32

FINDING ROY NEARY 34

THEY WERE INVITED 36

THE FINAL PIECES 40

CHOICES 42

THE FIVE NOTES 44

LAST WRITES? 46

PART TWO

DEVILS TOWER (MAY 17–28, 1976) 50

MOBILE, ALABAMA (MAY 29–SEPTEMBER 2, 1976) 58

LEAVING RELIANCE 64

HOME SWEET HOME 68

LANGUAGE BARRIERS 74

MEET THE GUILERS 78

THE BIG SET 84

SHOOTING THE "GRAND" CANYON 92

TECHNICAL DIFFICULTIES / NATURE CALLS 96

A CHANGE OF VENUE 100

WELCOME TO EARTH 102

THE "GRAYS" 104

THE RETURNEES (AUGUST 5–18, 1976) 108

MEET THE ALIENS 112

WHAT ARE WE LOOKING AT? 118

CRESCENDO SUMMIT (AUGUST 19–SEPTEMBER 2, 1976) 122

PART THREE

GOING "POST-AL" 128

CLOUDY WITH A CHANCE OF ETS 130

MATT'S MATTES 134

MODEL BEHAVIOR 142

A PASSAGE TO INDIA 146

THE MOTHER OF ALL SHIPS 152

SMOKING REQUIRED 164

BRIGHT LIGHTS AND SHOOTING STARS 166

ALTERED SPECIES 170

ONE MORE ROUND OF SHOOTING 174

PUBLIC ENCOUNTERS OF THE FIRST TIME 180

THE SPECIAL EDITION 182

WHEN YOU WISH UPON A STAR 188

ACKNOWLEDGMENTS 190

OPPOSITE The animatronic alien puppet created for the finale of *Close Encounters of the Third Kind* and affectionately dubbed "Puck" by Steven Spielberg.

FOREWORD

Close Encounters of the Third Kind has been part of my life from the time my father took me out—in the deepest black of night—to see the Perseid meteor shower.

For the first time, I opened my eyes and my mind to considering the possibility of the existence of life off our planet, and to the prospect that someday an alien civilization exploring the cosmos could pay us a visit.

Back then, and throughout the 1950s and '60s, there were continual reports of UFO sightings that scientists and government agencies worked in secret to investigate and possibly debunk. But among those were the 5 percent of sightings from credible witnesses that could never be explained.

Those sightings sparked my imagination and served as the genesis of the film we began to shoot in late 1975, two years before its release.

A film about our civilization's first contact with an extraterrestrial race presented huge challenges, not only to me as its writer-director but to all of us behind the production. One of the biggest: Where exactly would the final close encounter take place? We had spent months searching for a site that was intended to be at the base of a geological landmark when our production designer, Joe Alves, found Devils Tower in Wyoming. And it also took us months to find a converted hangar in Mobile, Alabama, that was ninety-five feet from floor to ceiling. It eventually housed what is still the largest indoor set ever constructed for any of my films. Other scenes took us to Mexico and India. Throughout this book, you will learn how our teams in every department turned my dream into my dream movie.

Forty years later, *Close Encounters* remains one of my most personal films. It's one of a very few movies that I not only directed but wrote, and when I started the script in 1973, I was still in my mid-twenties and hadn't yet directed my first feature. The very first scene I wrote was the very last in the movie—the encounter between extraterrestrials and mankind.

Close Encounters is a film in which space has several meanings, and so does light, whether it's the warm orange glow that envelops four-year-old Barry when he opens the door of his house, or the symphony of rays that pours down from the spaceships and the Mothership. The idea that we are not alone—the *hope* that we are not alone—is a theme I've returned to in several films since then, some frightening, some gentle. But the optimism of *Close Encounters* will always remain close to my heart.

Today, forty years after the film debuted, it's a special pleasure to know that new generations will be able to see it for the first time the way it was intended to be experienced—on colossal screens—and, with this book, to be able to invite you deeper into the journey we all took to bring you closer to *Close Encounters of the Third Kind*.

—Steven Spielberg
November 2017

BELOW Spielberg prepares Puck for his screen debut.
OPPOSITE The director sets up a shot at the base of Devils Tower in Wyoming.

INTRODUCTION

Close Encounters of the Third Kind is one of the most unique Hollywood blockbusters in the history of cinema. Like many of Steven Spielberg's films, it is filled with unforgettable, awe-inspiring moments, whether it's the sheer spectacle that marks the arrival of the Mothership or the comparatively simple, but no less effective, instant when young Barry Guiler's toys suddenly spring to life in the middle of the night. However, it is the film's unusual narrative drive that sets it apart as an achievement both magnificent and unconventional.

TOP The alien Mothership makes its entrance, rising from behind Devils Tower.

ABOVE UFOs approach the landing site at Devils Tower for their meeting with a group of human scientists.

OPPOSITE Promotional artwork for *Close Encounters* from Columbia Pictures.

Close Encounters is a film about the boundless possibilities of the universe and finding hope beyond our world. As such, the driving force of the plot is one man's unshakable belief that there is something out there. Unlike Spielberg's megahit *Jaws*, which debuted in 1975, two and a half years before *Close Encounters*, there's no villain lurking in the depths. If there's an enemy to be found at all in *Close Encounters*, it's the repercussions of being too enmeshed in the everyday world at the expense of the possibilities offered by the cosmos.

This lack of conventional movie plotting and focus on the power of imagination and vision gives *Close Encounters* a dreamlike quality that has more in common with European cinema than traditional Hollywood filmmaking. Nevertheless, *Close Encounters* struck a chord with the regular moviegoing public, becoming a smash-hit phenomenon on its release. At a time when ufology was at the height of its popularity, Spielberg's film permanently redefined how UFOs and alien beings were viewed in the popular imagination, the famous "five notes" of composer John Williams's score becoming forever associated with the arrival of visitors from other worlds.

The film's impact on pop culture extended to the way in which it perfected the themes that would become beloved cornerstones of Spielberg's filmmaking: an ordinary man thrown into an extraordinary situation; the importance of family and the messy reality of trying to keep one together; the sense of pure awe and the feeling that something magical is truly within our reach; and, perhaps most important, the notion that the forces of conformity cannot oppress the power of imagination.

Forty years after its release, *Close Encounters of the Third Kind* continues to enthrall and beguile, its hopeful message as timeless as its exemplary special effects. An intensely personal film for Spielberg, and one that tells you as much about the man as the filmmaker, *Close Encounters* was brought to the screen with the same unshakable sense of belief that compelled Roy Neary to seek out the Mothership. Like Neary's, Spielberg's path to fulfilling his vision would not be an easy one.

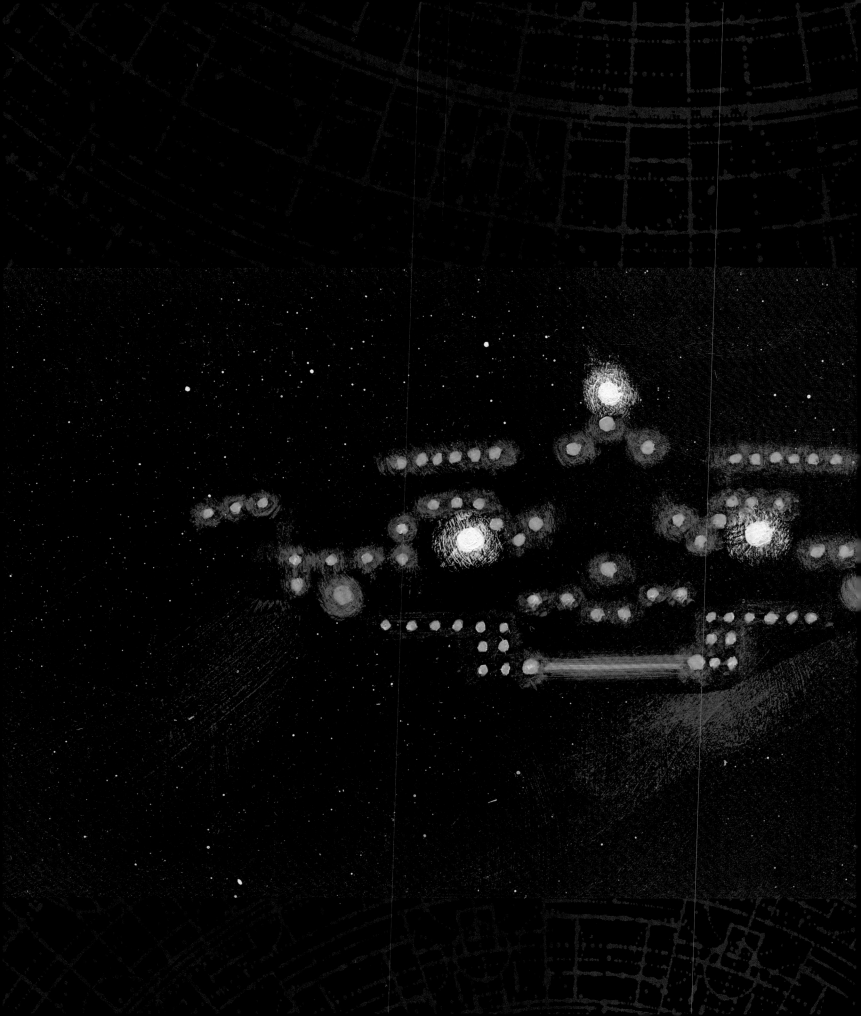

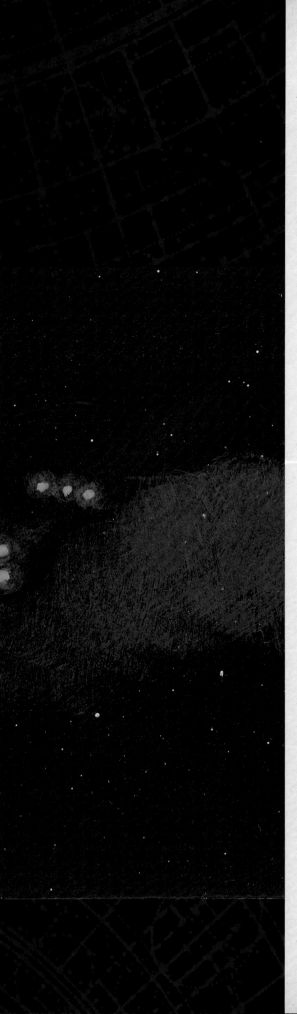

PART ONE

THEY CAME FROM BEYOND . . .

Throughout the late 1940s and early 1950s, the American public's interest in alien life grew exponentially. While sci-fi films, comics, and novels featuring beings from outer space had been popular during the 1930s and early 1940s, it was a landmark real-life incident in 1947 that ignited UFO mania like never before. On June 27 of that year, Kenneth Arnold, a businessman and private pilot, sighted what he described as nine objects soaring through the sky near Mount Rainier in Washington State. The US Civil Aeronautics Administration tried to explain his claims away, but the story was picked up by international wire services, and other residents from the area came forward to substantiate the sighting. The story triggered hundreds of UFO reports around the world, and soon the term "flying saucers" was coined for these mysterious objects in the sky.

The next month, it was reported that a "flying disc" had crashed in Roswell, New Mexico. US Air Force officials quickly sought to put an end to speculation about the incident, claiming that the object that crashed was actually a weather balloon. Like the Arnold incident, the Roswell episode fanned the flames of public interest, and UFO sightings continued to be reported on a regular basis. The sheer volume of those reports led to the formation of the US government agency Project Blue Book, a group focused on investigating and ultimately debunking UFO sightings.

While the American government was diligently working to deny that extraterrestrials were visiting our planet, Hollywood was taking full advantage of the public's fascination with visitors from other worlds. The 1950s saw a spate of films in which the denizens of Earth were the target of a wide variety of malevolent alien species. Intergalactic threats arrived in the form of *The Thing from Another World*, *It! The Terror from Beyond Space*, *Invaders from Mars*, *Killers from Space*, and *The Blob*. We also had to endure the *Invasion of the Body Snatchers* and *The War of the Worlds*, among countless others. Even Abbott and Costello and the Three Stooges had run-ins with otherworldly creatures.

One of the rare exceptions to the "us versus them" nature of the UFO genre was the 1951 classic *The Day the Earth Stood Still*, directed by Robert Wise. The hero of the film was Klaatu, an ostensibly benign alien who had come to Earth to deliver a message from the planets beyond: If humanity ever extends its warlike behavior into outer space, it will face obliteration at the hands of the intergalactic peacekeeping force he represents.

Whether humanity was facing outright invasion from beyond the stars or being threatened with total destruction by a well-meaning alien police force, in the extraterrestrial cinema of 1950s America, it didn't seem there was a great deal of hope in the heavens. For one young boy growing up in Haddon Township, New Jersey, however, outer space didn't represent a threat but rather a reason to be hopeful.

PAGES 10–11 A production painting by George Jensen depicts first contact between mankind and the alien emissaries.

LEFT An early production design sketch of the Mothership by George Jensen.

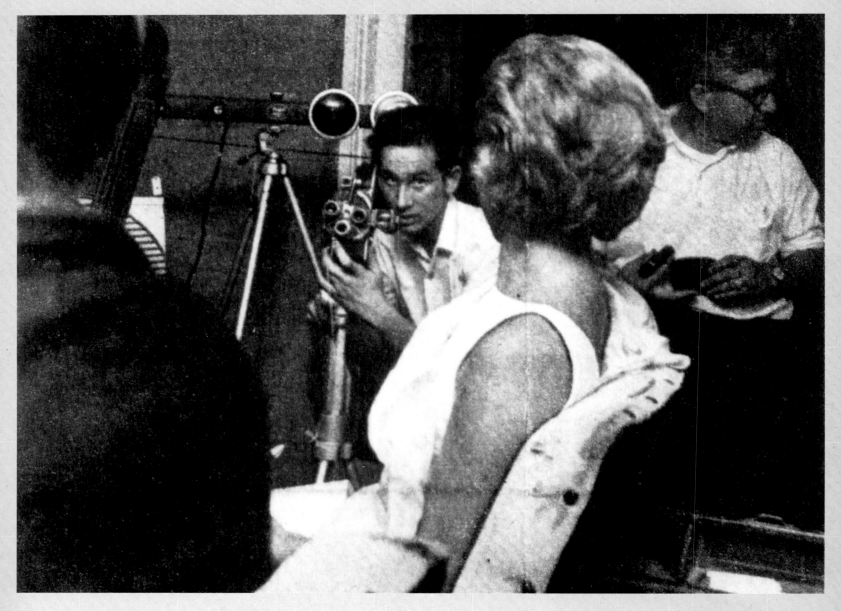

LOOKING TO THE SKIES

As the world around him indulged in its fixation on extraterrestrial life, a young Steven Spielberg had an experience that opened his imagination to the wonders of the cosmos. In the early 1950s, Arnold Spielberg woke up his young son in the middle of the night and drove him to a field where a group of people had assembled. Before they arrived, Spielberg recalls, his chief emotion was fear: "My dad kept saying it was a surprise, and the last time he said something was going to be a surprise, he promised to take me to a circus, and it turned out to be my first movie, *The Greatest Show on Earth*, which was *about* a circus, and that probably stuck in my craw somewhere."

Arriving at the field, Arnold spread out a blanket, and the two lay gazing at the night skies. "When we looked up, I saw my first shooting star," says Spielberg. "It turned out to be the Perseid meteor shower. I think there was a streak of light that burned through the sky every fifteen to thirty seconds, and I remember that being the first time I ever had a sense of wonder. Looking back, it was probably the greatest gift my dad ever gave me, next to my life."

After the outing, the elder Spielberg, an electrical engineer by trade, built a reflecting telescope, which further fueled Steven's interest in astronomy. "That was the first time I was able

to see the rings of Saturn and the moons of Jupiter," he recalls. "What I really got lost in were the craters on the moon. That was gobsmacking."

Several years later, at the age of sixteen, Spielberg combined his interest in the stars and his growing love of filmmaking when he wrote, directed, and composed the score for his first feature-length film, *Firelight*, which he shot in 8mm. Enlisting the aid of family, high school friends, and neighbors, he made the film in and around his Phoenix home (the Spielbergs had relocated from New Jersey in 1953). The story concerned a group of scientists (including a UFO believer) who investigate a series of lights in the sky and the

disappearance of a number of residents and their pets from a small Arizona town. Made at a cost of $500, *Firelight* was shown once at a local theater, where it sold out, earning the young filmmaker a small profit.

Interestingly, at the time, Spielberg's fascination with the stars served to offset his underlying sense of dread over the very ominous events occurring in the world around him. "I had that impression about the night sky, but I feared the day sky," he says. "I grew up during the Cold War, and I feared nuclear annihilation, as [did] most of my friends. We feared it even more as we got into our teenage years, and we realized that we came very close to the abyss during the Cuban Missile Crisis. During the day, I feared ICBMs [intercontinental ballistic missiles] raining down on our cities, and at night I only looked up at the skies with hope and wonder."

After moving to Southern California, where he studied various courses in the arts (including some rudimentary filmmaking classes) at California State University, Long Beach, Spielberg began his storied rise as a filmmaker. His award-winning short film *Amblin'* led to his first professional assignment as a director for Universal Television, where he honed his craft on episodes of popular series including *Marcus Welby, M.D.*, *The Name of the Game*, Rod Serling's *Night Gallery*, *Columbo*, and the acclaimed telefilm *Duel*.

Wanting to turn his attention to full-length feature films, Spielberg began developing a number of projects that he could direct. His first, *The Sugarland Express*, was inspired by the real-life story of a young Texas couple who took a state trooper hostage and led the police on a chase that would ultimately involve more than one hundred patrol cars. During filming,

Spielberg's mind drifted back to his interest in extraterrestrials and UFOs, and he decided to tackle the subject in his next film.

At the time, the United States was enmeshed in the Watergate scandal, which implicated President Richard Nixon in a break-in at the Democratic National Committee headquarters; when initially formulating the story for his UFO movie, Spielberg took inspiration from the cloak-and-dagger antics of the conspirators. In his earliest plot for the film, he envisioned the main character as a military officer who worked as a UFO debunker for Project Blue Book—until, that is, he has his own very real experience with a UFO. Forever changed by this encounter, he would use his insider position to uncover a government plot to keep the existence of extraterrestrials hidden from the public. The film would end with the arrival of the Mothership, a giant alien spacecraft far bigger than the UFO the protagonist encountered earlier in the story.

"I used to call it *A Meeting of the Minds*," says Spielberg. "Those were the themes I was exploring with government cover-ups, and the powers that be turning out to be not our heroes, but the enemy of the people. I thought that in order to protect the human race from panic, based on the truth of this encounter that was about to take place, the government would not only put a lid on the truth, but create all kinds of disinformation to put people off the trail of the truth. So it was a story about aliens and Watergate."

While Spielberg was preparing *The Sugarland Express* for release, he met producer Michael Phillips, who was working on postproduction for the Paul Newman–Robert Redford crime caper *The Sting*, along with his producing partner and then-wife, Julia Phillips. "We were

THESE PAGES A sixteen-year-old Steven Spielberg directs his first feature-length film, *Firelight*.

both on the [Universal] lot every day," recalls Michael Phillips. "We were contemporaries [of Spielberg's] and began to have lunch [with him] at the commissary, and discovered a mutual enthusiasm for science fiction, and *The Day the Earth Stood Still*."

This new kinship led Spielberg to approach the couple with an offer. "One day he said, 'I want to come out to the beach and talk to you and Julia about a new project,'" Phillips recalls. "We were already great fans of his work from *Duel*. He came out and said, 'I want you to produce a movie I want to make about UFOs and Watergate.' . . . We were great believers in him, we liked him, and thought, 'Why not?'"

"They were big-time producers," Spielberg notes, "about to win the Academy Award for *The Sting*. I sensed that Julia and Michael both, as a tag team, would be the best people to take my movie and get it produced. I felt safe with them. Julia was a force of nature, and Michael was the voice of reason. Julia was headstrong and Michael was heart-strong."

The Phillipses' first step was to find a studio that would develop and distribute the film. Unfortunately, Twentieth Century Fox turned them down because they already had a

sci-fi picture on their slate—*Star Wars*, directed by Spielberg's close friend George Lucas. Luckily, the husband-and-wife team's next stop proved to be much more productive.

In the early 1970s, Columbia Pictures had experienced a dramatic change of fortune. The once mighty studio was floundering under the weight of a number of high-priced productions that failed to attract audiences. As a result, the studio's stock price took a dive, and drastic measures were needed to keep it from sliding into bankruptcy. After a total shake-up of the board of directors, the new regime needed someone to head their motion picture division. Columbia chose David Begelman, who, along with Freddie Fields, had formed the highly influential talent agency Creative Management Associates, with clients including Judy Garland, Barbra Streisand, Steve McQueen, and Paul Newman. Julia Phillips had worked for Begelman years earlier and had a rapport with the new studio head that she felt would help them successfully pitch *Watch the Skies*—the new working title for Spielberg's UFO thriller—to Columbia.

The meeting went well. Begelman liked the premise and, given his considerable background

OPPOSITE On location, Spielberg frames a scene with producer Michael Phillips.

ABOVE Noted ufologist Dr. J. Allen Hynek, who coined the phrase "close encounters of the third kind."

BELOW Producers Michael and Julia Phillips.

in talent management, was shrewd enough to know that having the producers of *The Sting* and a promising young director like Steven Spielberg at the studio would only help to improve Columbia's public image. However, Begelman did have concerns about how much the film would cost.

"Before anyone else had a chance to answer, Steven tossed out a number," says Michael Phillips. "He said $2.7 to $2.9 million. We got outside the door, and we said, 'Where did you get that [number]? There's no script.' He said, 'I just had a sense that was the highest number he would go for.'"

More than forty years later, Spielberg has no recollection of ad-libbing a budget for Begelman's benefit. "If I gave a figure, it wasn't my being manipulative, and trying to advantage myself, by not giving the studio accurate estimates," he says. "I don't recall giving any figure to anyone, but if I did that, it was because I thought that was what the film would cost."

Either way, at the time Columbia had a strict edict that films with budgets in excess of $3 million would not be green-lit, and so Spielberg's estimate was just within their margin. The *Watch the Skies* team received a development deal. "We were just an interesting package, but worth only a small investment at the time," says Michael Phillips. Under the terms of the deal, Columbia would fund only the development of the script. If the studio was satisfied with the finished screenplay, it would continue to allot funds to continue the project

and finance the hiring of key department heads (production design, special effects, costume, etc.). Only when the screenplay and the final budget were approved would they commit to putting the film into full production. Throughout the preproduction stages, the studio had the right to shut the film down and either take the financial loss or put the project in turnaround (try to sell it to another studio to recoup the money they had already spent).

Putting together a winning screenplay that would gain Columbia's confidence was therefore the first priority. Spielberg had decided to lay out the bones of the story himself and then have another writer come in to create the first draft of the script. His first thought was to hire Matthew Robbins and Hal Barwood, with whom he had written *The Sugarland Express.* Unfortunately, the duo were working on their own science fiction story, *Clearwater,* which had been green-lit by another studio. When Robbins and Barwood reluctantly passed, Michael and Julia Phillips suggested another writer, who was promptly hired. However, when the first draft was delivered, Spielberg and the Phillipses agreed that it had strayed way too far from the director's original vision, and they chose not to pursue a rewrite.

While the search for a new writer commenced, Spielberg immersed himself in UFO research, an endeavor that led to a title change for the project. One book in particular had a major impact on the director, *The UFO*

Experience: A Scientific Enquiry, written in 1972 by Dr. J. Allen Hynek, one of the top UFO experts (or "ufologists") in the United States. Originally a member of Project Blue Book, Hynek started out as a skeptic of the UFO reports he had been assigned to investigate. However, while many of the accounts were outlandish and easily dismissed, some were submitted by credible sources. In addition, many of the reports were filled with a remarkable amount of detail that corresponded to other accounts drawn from all over the world. After intense analysis by Hynek and his team, many of these accounts remained unexplainable, and deserving of deeper investigation. "He himself became a convert," says Spielberg. "He began to believe the government was covering things up, even from him, their chief debunker."

After Project Blue Book was shut down, Hynek continued to scientifically analyze UFO cases. In his book he outlines three classifications for the different types of experiences witnesses had reported:

CLOSE ENCOUNTER OF THE FIRST KIND—"Visual sightings of an unidentified flying object seemingly less than five hundred feet away that show an appreciable angular extension and considerable detail."

CLOSE ENCOUNTER OF THE SECOND KIND—"A UFO event in which a physical effect is alleged. This can be interference in the functioning of a vehicle or electronic device; animals reacting; a physiological effect such as paralysis or heat and discomfort in the witness; or some physical trace like impressions in the ground, scorched or otherwise affected vegetation, or a chemical trace."

CLOSE ENCOUNTER OF THE THIRD KIND—"UFO encounters in which an animated creature is present. These include humanoids, robots, and humans who seem to be occupants or pilots of a UFO."

It was, of course, the third category that Spielberg deemed a perfect title for his project. However, when Columbia Pictures announced the upcoming release of a new movie called *Close Encounters of the Third Kind*, Hynek contacted the studio informing them that they were infringing on his work. Spielberg had been unaware that Hynek had created the phrase and thought it to be part of the public lexicon. Eager to resolve the situation, Spielberg contacted Hynek personally to discuss the matter, and would later invite him to join the production as a technical adviser. The ufologist soon gave his blessing for the title and would take Spielberg up on his offer to become part of the team.

As the filmmakers continued their quest for a new screenwriter, Spielberg received an unexpected call that would take his focus away from *Close Encounters*. Producers Richard D. Zanuck and David Brown, who were already in preproduction on their killer-shark thriller *Jaws*, called to tell him that there had been "creative differences" with the director they had originally hired, and asked if Spielberg would take the helm. Spielberg accepted the assignment, and it was decided a writer would be hired for *Close Encounters* who could spend time with Spielberg on location for *Jaws*, where they could discuss the script during the director's downtime.

Screenwriter John Hill, whose only previous writing credit was the made-for-television drama *Griffin and Phoenix* (starring Peter Falk and Jill Clayburgh), was brought on board and traveled to Martha's Vineyard, Massachusetts, with Michael and Julia Phillips to spend a weekend with Spielberg. Once he was on the *Jaws* set, he found that the extreme challenges plaguing the production, including a malfunctioning mechanical shark, would leave the director with precious little spare time. Hill would ultimately get just one meeting with Spielberg and the producers, but it was enough to hash out the

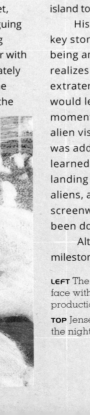

overall framework of the story, and he left the island to begin writing.

His first draft reflected Spielberg's initial key story points, including the protagonist being an Air Force officer/UFO debunker who realizes he is a pawn in the government's extraterrestrial cover-up, a situation that would lead to his being present for a momentous meeting between mankind and alien visitors. In one key plot element that was added at this point, the protagonist learned the location of the Mothership's landing site via telepathic contact with the aliens, a suggestion offered to Spielberg by screenwriter and friend John Milius, who had been doing some rewrite work on *Jaws*.

Although Hill followed Spielberg's plot milestones closely, the director and his

LEFT The hero of Spielberg's story comes face-to-face with extraterrestrials in this concept art by production illustrator George Jensen.

TOP Jensen's illustration of a UFO streaking through the night skies.

producing partners were not satisfied with the resulting script, feeling that it didn't convey the necessary joy and wonder at the heart of the story. Fortunately, the script did serve one very important purpose: It convinced Spielberg that he would have to write this deeply personal story himself.

"I wasn't looking for a stenographer," explains Spielberg. "I was looking for a writer with independent thoughts and imagination. But after several frustrating attempts by writers to put my vision down in screenplay form, I realized the only way I was going to be able to express these thoughts was to go through the painful process of writing it myself. I was just trying to get writers to write my story, but a writer has to write their own."

Although famed for his expansive imagination and boundless creativity, Spielberg has never been a fan of the writing process itself. "My reluctance is the reluctance that any writer has—sitting down and focusing on something," he says. "For me to write a screenplay requires the energy it takes me to direct three movies back to back. I have not written a lot of scripts. It's that labor intensive for me."

Another important lesson learned from the two previous scripts was that the Watergate-inspired governmental cover-up angle was starting to feel a little tired.

This notion was further confirmed when, during the *Jaws* shoot, Spielberg spoke with veteran NBC news anchorman John Chancellor, who had a summer home on Martha's Vineyard, about the concept. "I was telling Chancellor . . . [about] my UFO Watergate movie," says Spielberg. "Chancellor said, 'Don't you think if the UFO phenomenon was real, that Nixon, in his desperation to stay in office, would have reached for any smokescreen to have led the press in a different direction, and away from Watergate and the crimes that were being committed? Don't you think he would have told the world that aliens are here?' That threw the biggest bucket of cold water on my movie that I hadn't even directed yet!"

Spielberg decided to come at the story from a different perspective, one with which he was more comfortable. "He really cut loose all the shackles," comments Michael Phillips, "and made a Spielberg type of movie: ordinary family, extraordinary situation."

The director had always wanted to present his aliens in a peaceful, benevolent way, but he was a little nervous about how audiences would react now that he was removing the traditional thriller elements of the original story. "I think Steven was concerned we lacked a conventional villain, an antagonist, and [without that] how can we have a feeling of triumph at the end?" Phillips says. "That was the argument we went around on very briefly, before ultimately becoming comfortable with the lack of a villain."

The absence of a threat in the narrative was very much a product of Spielberg's personal viewpoint about life from other worlds, informed by his early experiences with stargazing. "I didn't look up in the sky thinking there was bad out there. I looked up at the cosmos, thinking there were wonderful mysteries to be discovered," he says. "[Astronomy] did not leave me with the impression that out there lived enemies of our planet. I guess I was brought up to believe that a civilization of higher intelligence would only travel this distance to explore and discover and not to annihilate and eradicate."

SPIELBERG'S FIRST DRAFT

Spielberg began the writing process for *Close Encounters* in the spring of 1975, while working on the final edit of *Jaws*. His first rough draft would contain a number of central plot points that would make it into the final film. The story centered on Norman Greenhouse, a foreman for the Indiana Power and Light Company who's called upon to deal with a massive power outage in the fictional Tolono County. The other main characters included a young single mother named Jillian Guiler and her four-year-old son, Barry, along with Robert Lacombe, the leader of an international team of scientists trying to make contact with visitors from another galaxy.

TOP Preproduction art shows Norman (who would later become Roy) and Jillian discovering the scientific complex as UFOs approach.

ABOVE AND OPPOSITE BOTTOM George Jensen production illustrations show the arrival of the aliens at the scientific installation.

OPPOSITE TOP Jillian takes photos of the aliens as Norman watches.

In his investigation of the blackout, Norman has his first encounter with a number of UFOs, an incident that leaves him obsessed with finding out more about the phenomenon. Jillian Guiler and her son are visited as well, and she experiences a similar reaction, a calling that we will later learn has been implanted in the minds of those who encounter the alien visitors. Norman's report about his experiences is dismissed by the local Air Force authorities, and he also faces the derision of his neighbors and is fired from his job. His growing obsession leads to behavior that alarms his wife and children, who are ultimately driven away as Norman descends deeper and deeper into what seems to be total madness.

Norman and Jillian are both thunderstruck when they separately see a TV news report about a small town being evacuated by the Army. In the background of the report, "Wamsutter Mountain" is visible, an image that has been dominating their thoughts since they first came into contact with the UFOs. Norman travels to the location and ends up being taken into custody by the armed forces supervising the town's evacuation. He is interrogated by Lacombe, who realizes that Norman has been "invited" to the area by the ETs. Lacombe tries to convince the military that Norman should be allowed to stay, but Greenhouse is escorted onto a helicopter for evacuation. On board, Norman is surprised to see that Jillian, who traveled independently to Wamsutter Mountain, is also in the process of being forcibly removed from the site, along with several other people who were telepathically summoned by the visitors. Before the chopper can take off, Norman leads an escape attempt. Only he, Jillian and another man are able to reach the forested area around the base of the mountain, while the others are taken back into custody by the military. As the trio make their ascent, Wild Bill, the Army officer in charge of the operation, sends up helicopters loaded with nerve gas to subdue the escapees. Norman and Jillian barely make it safely to the top, but their new companion ends up as a casualty of the gas.

decides to stay secluded. When he sets foot on the landing strip floor, he notices a group of men being given last rites by a priest. Lacombe spies Norman in the midst of all the personnel, and brings him to the fore. As the musical interchange ends, a hatch in the Mothership opens and dozens of humanoid aliens emerge, exploring their surroundings and interacting with the people who have come to welcome them. Soon after, the men who were given their last rites walk slowly toward the craft. Norman joins them, and is immediately surrounded by the aliens, who take him by the hands and guide him into their ship.

As the story ends, Jillian, camera in hand, snaps picture after picture as the craft ascends back into the heavens.

Once over the ridge, the two descend into a valley, and are overwhelmed to discover an immense scientific installation, buzzing with activity and anticipation. The lights dim, and those assembled look to the skies. Norman and Jillian witness the arrival of a number of UFOs, which fly overhead, lighting up the canyon. Three of them hover over the site, seemingly assessing those in attendance. Lacombe signals a man stationed behind a Moog synthesizer, who taps out a series of notes, to which the ships flash their lights in response. Suddenly, rising up from behind the mountain, the Mothership appears. The notes are played again, and the Mothership responds by filling the night air with the exact same notes. Music becomes the first communication between the earthlings and the aliens.

As the Mothership lands, Norman climbs down to get a closer look, while Jillian

‒ ‒ ‒ ‒

While Spielberg was far from satisfied with this rough first draft, he felt it hit all the major beats he was aiming to cover in the film and felt confident enough to show it to Columbia. The response was positive, and so he proceeded to the second draft as preproduction on *Close Encounters of the Third Kind* slowly rumbled to life. However, Columbia had still not granted the official green light to the project, and so its future remained in the balance.

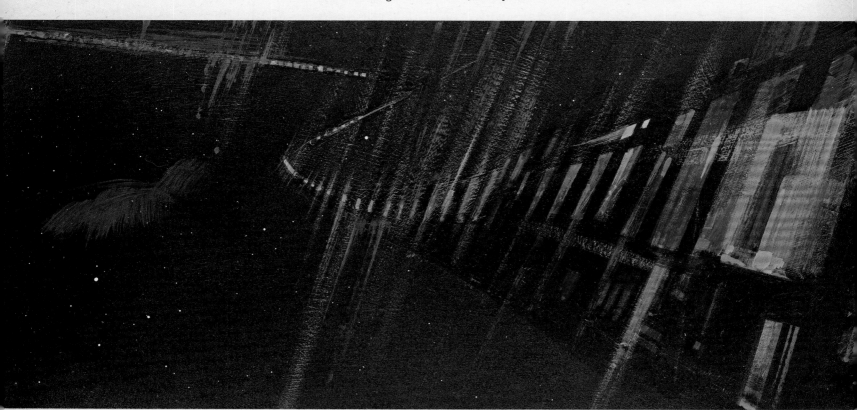

TWO ROADS DIVERGED

Although Spielberg wanted *Close Encounters* to be his next film, he remained open to the possibility of accepting another directorial assignment before *Jaws* hit theaters, especially as Columbia had not yet fully committed to *Close Encounters*. One such offer came from Universal Pictures, who sent him a script entitled *The Bingo Long Traveling All-Stars & Motor Kings*, a period piece about a group of baseball players who break away from the Negro League to form their own team, and embark on a barnstorming tour through the Midwest. Spielberg agreed to take on the film.

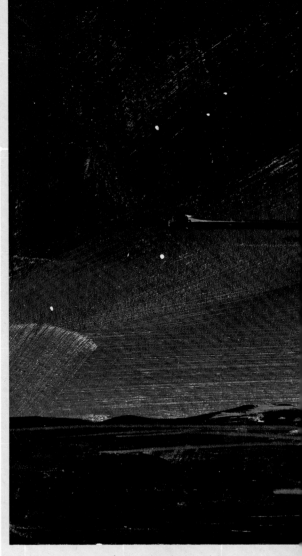

As the contracts were being prepared by Universal, Spielberg had production designer Joe Alves, who had worked on both *The Sugarland Express* and *Jaws*, begin research on the period in which the film was set. Having put together some materials, Alves invited Spielberg for a weekend at a cabin in Mammoth Lakes, California, where they could discuss the film. During their time together, the conversation strayed from baseball to UFOs. "He started talking to me about Hynek's book and *Close Encounters of the Third Kind*," says Alves. Although the production designer liked the *Bingo Long* project, he confessed that the premise of *Close Encounters* sounded like a much more intriguing and exciting film. "He told me he didn't have a final deal yet, but he and Michael and Julia Phillips were trying to make it work," says Alves. "We went back to LA, and I didn't hear from him. A couple of weeks later, I got a call from [director] John Badham, with whom I did a number of television things, and he said he was [directing] *Bingo Long*." Spielberg had decided to go back to his original plan.

"I got out of it just as quickly as I got into it," says Spielberg. "It might have been a dalliance

on my part. It was about a time in American baseball that I was unfamiliar with, and as I did research, I became very compelled by that story, but *Close Encounters* erased a lot of films that I had flirted with and I really couldn't make another film until I made *Close Encounters*. I would have waited another two or three years, and probably would have flirted and semi-committed to three or four other films, but I knew I couldn't move my life forward until *Close Encounters* was behind me."

Not long after hearing from John Badham, Alves received another call, this time from John Veitch, a Columbia Pictures executive, who confirmed that *Close Encounters* was inching forward. Alves recalls that "John said, 'Well, we're putting together this movie. Steven's off doing promotions for *Jaws*, and I've got a local production manager doing some kind of budget. Here's how it's going to work. We're going to shoot everything on the [studio] lot, and down the street on Warner's back lot, but we need to find an interesting mountain. So you can go off and find that mountain.' And they put me on salary."

"I wrote the monolith [dubbed Wamsutter Mountain] in the script, but I didn't

have a location [in mind]," says Spielberg. "I just said it was a butte, but also something that was unmistakable . . . I needed something that could become a visual MacGuffin, and a kind of talisman that would be envisioned by everybody who had been contacted to come to this rendezvous. I just didn't know where it was. I thought about Monument Valley, but John Ford owns Monument Valley, and I wasn't going to go there, so I sent Joe to go off and find a place."

Alves hit the road, searching for a unique butte that would serve as the first meeting place for mankind and visitors from another world. His extensive expedition spanned the North American continent, and he would clock more than 3,500 miles, his first stop being Rapid City, South Dakota, where he explored the landscape behind Mount Rushmore. Among his other stops were iconic locations such as Utah's Bryce Canyon, Chimney Rock in Nebraska, and Shiprock in New Mexico. The production designer took dozens of photographs of each location, and upon his return to Los Angeles he would manually tape the photos together into giant panoramas to show to Spielberg and the producers.

In the process of researching potential locations, Alves started chatting with *Jaws* screenwriter Carl Gottlieb about his travels. "He was looking at the map, and he said 'You know, I went to this place, Devils Tower, when I was younger,' recalls Alves. "'That's a pretty interesting place.'" Alves put it on the list.

Composed of igneous rock, and situated in northeast Wyoming near the town of Hulett, Devils Tower rises 1,267 feet above the Belle Fourche River and was declared a national monument by President Theodore Roosevelt in 1906. As Alves first drove toward the imposing butte, he was struck by its sudden and dramatic appearance. "At Shiprock and some of the others, you see them from miles away as you approach them," Alves says. "Here, you're driving and you see this little thing sticking up, and then it disappears. Then you continue to drive, and then it's bigger. When it appeared next, my reaction was 'Oh my God!' To me it was like a religious thing."

When he showed Spielberg his assembled Devils Tower panorama, the director knew immediately that it was the exact location he was looking for.

25

THE NEXT STEP

Following its release on June 20, 1975, *Jaws* would quickly become the highest-grossing film of all time (it would be eclipsed two years later by *Star Wars*). Its huge success was a welcome surprise not only for Spielberg, but for Columbia Pictures as well. Although Columbia still wasn't ready to green-light production on *Close Encounters*, the significance of having Spielberg's follow-up to *Jaws* on their release schedule was not lost on the studio, and so progress on the project began to pick up pace.

Spielberg was given the go-ahead to assemble the key members of his team. In addition to Joe Alves, he recruited several others with whom he had worked on his two previous films. Hungarian-born cinematographer Vilmos Zsigmond had come to Spielberg's attention with his work on Robert Altman's *McCabe & Mrs. Miller*, which led to their first collaboration, on *The Sugarland Express*. A previous commitment had kept Zsigmond from shooting *Jaws,* but when he got the call for *Close Encounters*, he was excited to be reunited with Spielberg. "Vilmos was one of the great artists of my generation as a cinematographer," says Spielberg. "From *McCabe & Mrs. Miller* to *Deliverance* to *Heaven's Gate*, which is one of the most brilliantly photographed movies ever, to Michael Cimino's other movie *The Deer Hunter*. When I asked him to photograph *Sugarland*, I quite frankly could not believe he would say yes to a first-time director."

Composer John Williams had also first worked with Spielberg on *The Sugarland Express,* and went on to create one of the most recognizable themes in the history of cinema for *Jaws,* winning both an Oscar and a Golden Globe for his work. His contribution to *Close Encounters* would be no less iconic. "I was crazy about the whole idea," he says. "The idea of contact with the life that we know is out there, in some form, is an irresistible attraction for any artist working in any medium."

Other key personnel who came from the *Jaws* crew included Shari Rhodes (casting director), Charlsie Bryant (script supervisor), and Roy Arbogast (physical effects).

To create the film's visual effects, Columbia wanted to bring in the former head of their special effects department, Lawrence W. Butler, an Academy Award winner whose career spanned dozens of films including *Casablanca, Destination Tokyo,* and *Marooned.* Spielberg had great respect for Butler's body of work, but as the veteran explained some of the tried-and-tested techniques he thought could be used in the film, the director began to doubt that the results would achieve the level of wonder he sought to evoke.

For Spielberg, the movies of filmmakers George Pal and Stanley Kubrick were benchmarks in sci-fi moviemaking and, like his heroes, he fully intended to push the limits of what visual effects could achieve for *Close Encounters*. The thrilling sci-fi adventures *Destination Moon* (1950), *When Worlds Collide* (1951), and *The War of the Worlds* (1953)—all produced by Pal—were credited with bringing a new level of realism to the sci-fi genre, while director Kubrick's thoughtful masterpiece *2001: A Space Odyssey* (1968) became an instant classic and featured stunning Oscar-winning effects. "They are certainly of two minds and styles," Spielberg says of the filmmakers. "George Pal was straight down the middle, a Hollywood science fiction visionary, and Kubrick was intellectual and esoteric and a visionary genius. They were the extremes of how I had hoped *Close Encounters* would fall into some kind of cinematic lexicon if the film turned out to be any good."

In order for Spielberg to fulfill his vision for the film, he knew he would need a visual effects expert whose abilities went far beyond the standards of the industry at the time. As such, he turned to one of the key minds behind the effects on Kubrick's masterpiece. While most of the technicians who had worked on *2001: A Space Odyssey* were based in London, Douglas Trumbull, one of the film's visual effects supervisors, was a resident of Southern California. However, Spielberg was unsure if Trumbull would be interested in working on his film since the visual effects whiz had branched into directing with the sci-fi feature *Silent Running*, and had recently turned down an offer from George Lucas to create the effects for *Star Wars*.

Spielberg reached out anyway, and found that Trumbull was indeed enmeshed in a number of projects. "I was under contract to Paramount Pictures with my company Future General, where I was making terrific headway in developing a whole new frame rate, 70mm movie process, ultra-scan, simulation rides, new cameras, and new means of real-time digital composing, and all kinds of things that were very interesting to me at the time," Trumbull explains. "Unfortunately, Paramount had gone through a big management change, and totally lost interest in what I was doing, and was starting not to fund forward progress on it. When Steven came along and asked if I would do the effects, I requested Paramount's permission for a loan-out agreement, because this [job] would further my activities to acquire equipment and develop all kinds of other things that I thought were important parts of my long-term vision for movie technology."

Beyond the technological opportunities the *Close Encounters* job would afford him, and more important, were Trumbull's impressions of both the director and the film's subject matter. "I've been a UFO fan all my life," he says.

ABOVE Spielberg with composer John Williams.

OPPOSITE TOP Spielberg reviews footage with special effects wizard Douglas Trumbull.

OPPOSITE BOTTOM Spielberg with film editor Michael Kahn.

"I grew up with UFOs on the cover of magazines like *Life*, *Newsweek*, *Time*, and *Popular Mechanics*. The 1940s and '50s was a humongous time of UFO sightings and commentary. I was fascinated with the whole subject, and when I read the screenplay, I thought it seemed very informed and intelligent, and an optimistic take on the whole idea of an alien encounter . . . It really resonated with me because I thought at the time, and I still believe today, that there's every reason to believe that there's been [an alien-humankind] contact situation going on for hundreds, if not thousands, of years."

Another newcomer to the Spielberg camp was film editor Michael Kahn. Verna Fields, who edited *Jaws*, had been the director's first choice to cut *Close Encounters*, but she had taken a studio job as vice president of feature production at Universal. Spielberg set out to find a replacement, meeting with no fewer than twenty editors in his quest to find the right person for the job. During his meeting with Kahn, the two started out discussing the film but soon digressed. "We started talking, and we discovered that we were both Boy Scouts—not only Eagle Scouts, but we were both members of the Order of the Arrow in scouting," recalls Spielberg. "We stopped talking about film and we started talking about scouting, and I just knew I had found my brother."

He continues, "The most intimate relationship for me in the motion picture process is in the editing room, because in the editing room you don't have to answer a thousand questions a day, you don't have a schedule and a budget chasing you up a hill and toward the cliff." Spielberg adds, "It's almost a time to meditate, and it's a time to relax with all the pieces we've amassed during my production. It's a beautiful time, and you want to spend it with somebody you really get along with."

DESIGNING A BIGGER "BOX"

Having established Devils Tower as the location for the finale of *Close Encounters*, Spielberg and Joe Alves began to discuss the design for the scientific installation/landing site that would come to be known as "Box Canyon." "In the script it said 'military encampment,' but that wasn't very exciting," says Alves. Before Devils Tower had been set as the location for the scene, Spielberg had actually suggested that the Mothership land between two fast-food restaurants. After being shown a quick mock-up of that setting, the director immediately dismissed the idea. Their further discussions led them to the idea that the landing site could be constructed like a sports arena–style complex. Rather than draw up sketches of his ideas for the set, Alves built a detailed tabletop model.

While Alves embarked on building the miniature version of the arena-style landing site, John Veitch at Columbia Pictures suggested using Stages 15 and 16 on the Burbank Studios lot—a facility shared by Columbia and Warner Bros.—for the live-action shooting of the scene. The two stages were attached, and the wall that separated them could be removed to create one enormous space, as had been done during filming of the extravagant 1967 musical *Camelot*. Alves began to build his prototype with that space in mind, and soon the model expanded to the point where it almost filled his trailer. As he continued to work on it, Spielberg, Michael and Julia Phillips, and a number of Columbia executives would often visit to watch the progress. When asked what he thought of the model, Alves would reply, "I think it should be bigger, like twice as wide and twice as long." His visitors agreed, and ultimately the final mock-up became so expansive and detailed that Spielberg was able to use it to plan the shooting of a number of scenes.

Unfortunately, the model had grown so much that when Alves checked out the soundstages that Veitch suggested, he found the space to be inadequate. There were immovable structural columns that would prevent Spielberg from getting the dynamic shots he was planning, and even if there were a way to remove the visual obstacles, it still wasn't a big enough space. After some research, it was determined that no soundstage in Los Angeles (or in the world) was large enough to accommodate the needs of the filmmakers.

But shooting the scenes in an outdoor location would not be an option. Working on such a tight budget, Spielberg couldn't risk running into delays caused by inclement weather. An outdoor location would also mean logistical problems in terms of providing power for lighting and other necessary elements of a shoot. And shooting at night over a protracted period would take a toll on the cast and crew. The filmmakers needed an indoor space where they could control all the elements.

To solve the problem, Alves and production manager/line producer Clark Paylow looked into the possibility of shooting in World War II–era aircraft hangars, which they thought might have the extensive contained space they needed. "We went to Colorado, North Carolina, and Tillamook, Oregon," says Alves. "They had these gigantic hangars, but half of them were [then owned by] lumber companies, and you could hear the saws going all day. That wasn't going to work." After traveling to a number of hangars that turned out to be inadequate, Alves heard that the Brookley Air Force Base in Mobile, Alabama, might be workable and hopped on a plane to investigate.

The base was established in 1938 to maintain, supply, overhaul, and transport the nation's fleet of fighter aircraft. One of its many hangars was also designed to house

dirigibles, and it was this suitably vast space that caught Alves's attention. The structure measured 300 feet by 300 feet and rose over nine stories tall. While the height and width were satisfactory, the production needed it to be at least 450 feet long to house the entirety of the planned set. To address the issue, Alves planned to open the hangar doors at one end of the structure, thereby extending the length of the space.

While the production had originally planned to film at only one major out-of-town location, Devils Tower in Wyoming, they updated the schedule to include shooting time in Alabama.

With two locations locked, the production team was still making plans to shoot Norman Greenhouse's home and neighborhood in the Los Angeles area. However, Joe Alves strongly felt that the homes in Southern California had a distinct look that didn't mesh with the story and characters in the script. "In Indiana and those areas, people don't fence everything off," he says. "One piece of property runs to the other. In LA, they put up fences." When Alves expressed his concern to Clark Paylow, the line producer agreed to take a trip with him to explore location possibilities. They traveled to Indiana, where Spielberg's script took place, to find a community that was more in line with the kind of Midwestern aesthetic that Alves wanted. Knowing that it would make financial and scheduling sense to film everything in Alabama, they then went to Mobile to find similar communities. When they returned to Los Angeles and presented their findings to Spielberg, the director agreed that Mobile could indeed stand in for Indiana, and suggested they

go to the studio to see if the executives would consent, which they ultimately did.

As more and more of the filming was relegated to Wyoming and Alabama, it was ultimately decided to go "full location" for all the live action, with only the visual effects work to be created back in Southern California. Brookley Air Force Base had plenty of office space for the various production departments, and another huge hangar adjacent to the first one, where Alves could house another large set, as well as some of Douglas Trumbull's oversize visual effects equipment.

CONT. 2ND UFO SWEEPS OVER HEAD,.

JILL & BARRY JUMP ASIDE

SWERVING, NEARY SMASHES MAILBOXES

THESE PAGES Storyboards from the Crescendo Summit scene by George Jensen.

O UFO SHOOTS

THE SECOND DRAFT

While the full crew was being assembled and Alves worked on designing the sets for both the Wyoming and Alabama locations, Spielberg worked on the second draft of the script. Dated September 19, 1975, this version of the screenplay kept the same basic story, but incorporated a number of important changes that added more depth and backstory to the characters, as well as a few scenes which established that Earth had previously been visited by the ETs.

Robert Lacombe became Claude Lacombe, as Spielberg wanted the UFO group to have more of an international feel. As Lacombe spoke little English, the character of his translator, unnamed as yet but referred to as having a "heavy Brooklyn accent," was added, as well as a number of other assorted military types.

Jillian Guiler was given much more of a presence, first meeting Norman at Crescendo Summit, a UFO-watching hot spot in the Indiana countryside, amidst a gathering of the SPIWGOAH: The Society for the People Interested in What's Going On Around Here. It is at this location that Jillian talks to Norman about her first encounter with the UFOs and reveals that these visits have been going on for several weeks. In this draft, she leaves Barry in the care of her father while she makes her pilgrimage to Wamsutter Mountain.

After his meeting with a dismissive Major Benchley (a nod to *Jaws* novelist Peter Benchley) at Pease Air Force Base, the frustrated Norman spies a master circuit panel that controls the building's lighting. He flips a few switches, and as he drives away, a crowd gathers to see his handiwork. Norman has turned on the lights in a number of specific windows at the front of the building and darkened others, forming a message: "What remains," the screenplay says,

"spells 'UFO' across the entire face of the Pease Air Force Administration Facility."

Two scenes were added in which Lacombe and his group travel to distant locations and make startling discoveries. Hacking their way through a dense jungle in Brazil using machetes, they come to a perfectly flat clearing, one hundred yards in circumference. In the center of the clearing stand five World War II Navy Grumman torpedo bombers, collectively known as Flight 19—which in real life had disappeared during a training mission over the Bermuda Triangle in 1945—looking as fresh and shiny as when they first left the factory. In the midst of the Gobi Desert in Mongolia, the team discovers a 425-foot freighter lying on its side against the flattened dunes. The SS *Marine Sulphur Queen* had been reported missing en route from Beaumont, Texas, to Norfolk, Virginia, in 1963.

- - - -

The second draft of *Close Encounters* was tighter, more engaging, and, crucially, far more expansive than the previous version of the script. While it marked an important evolution in Spielberg's story, the increased budget it required would soon become a major sticking point with Columbia Pictures.

CRESCENDO SUMMIT
3RD SEQ.
EST. SHOT HILL FULL OF PEOPLE
ANGLE 8
LANDSCAPE 1

GOING "GREEN"

Even though the official green light had not yet been given, the extensive prep for the film began in the fall of 1975, and it was determined that shooting would likely begin in May of 1976. However, as the year neared its end, Columbia realized that in order to qualify for funds from tax shelters, and to be able to write off losses for the fiscal year, they would need to shoot at least one scene before the New Year. With no actors cast or sets built, the scene would have to be shot in a practical location, and could not feature any of the main characters.

As such, the decision was made to film one of the opening scenes from Spielberg's second draft, which featured a group of air traffic controllers in communication with a pilot who is being confronted midair by a UFO. The scene was shot at an air traffic control facility in Palmdale, California, on December 29 and 30, 1975, with local actors cast as the personnel. As 1976 was ushered in, *Close Encounters of the Third Kind* had its first shot in the can.

The beginning of 1976 also brought a change in the executive ranks at Columbia Pictures. Peter Guber, who had been the head of production at the time *Close Encounters* was brought to the studio, left the company to produce his own films. His replacement was Stanley Jaffe, who would report to chairman of the board David Begelman. Jaffe had been a studio executive at Paramount, and, as an independent producer, been responsible for films such as *Goodbye, Columbus* and *The Bad News Bears*. By the time Jaffe came aboard, the projected budget of *Close Encounters* had risen to somewhere in the range of $8 million to $10 million after Spielberg's second-draft additions. Unsurprisingly, his first meetings with the filmmakers were focused primarily on the budget.

"We met with Steven and Julia to try and bring down the costs," Jaffe remembers. "Anytime you work with a filmmaker and say, 'We want to have you spend less,' you're going to meet with resistance."

That said, despite the escalating budget of

Close Encounters, there were many reasons to be positive about its prospects. "There weren't a lot of films in the hopper when I got there," Jaffe says. "There just weren't that many scripts we had any interest in pursuing beyond where they were. Steven represented a film-maker we all respected, and it was a picture I thought was potentially a really terrific movie."

As the weeks passed, the studio still dragged its feet on giving the green light, a situation that had huge implications for the crew already working on the film.

Joe Alves desperately needed approval on a black tarp for the dirigible hangar set that would help extend it to 450 feet and provide the dark backing needed to create the illusion that the Box Canyon scenes were taking place at night. Alves went to Julia Phillips to request money for the backing. "She said, 'All right, just rent it,'" he recalls. "I said, 'No, I'm going to need a *mile* of black tarp, and it's going to take this company in Texas three months to make.' I had to have an answer or we couldn't move forward."

The other departments were in the same position as Alves, frozen in their progress until they had more money with which to proceed. Frustrated by the delays, Julia Phillips called a meeting with the top Columbia executives to plead their case.

Shortly after, the studio took the plunge, and the light turned from yellow to green. The official budget of *Close Encounters of the Third Kind* was approved at $11,889,259, almost four times Columbia's fiscal limit for new projects.

LEFT Julia Phillips with Steven Spielberg.

ABOVE The first scene filmed for *Close Encounters*, shot in an air traffic control facility in Palmdale, California.

FINDING ROY NEARY

With preproduction now in full swing, the task of casting the film came into focus. During the shooting of *Jaws*, Richard Dreyfuss, who played that film's resident shark expert, Matt Hooper, had seen Spielberg meeting with various Columbia executives about *Close Encounters*. "I remember saying to Steven, 'So, what's going on?'" says the actor. "He told me the general idea of *Watch the Skies*. At that time he told me it was [written] for like [a] Gene Hackman [type], a lifer in the Army. I was very intrigued, but I didn't possess [that kind of background]." After months of work on location, the *Jaws* production moved back to Los Angeles, where they shot a number of sequences in a water tank at the studio. "We'd shoot all night, and then we'd go to Steven's office in the morning, where he would work on *Close Encounters*," continues Dreyfuss. "I'd come with him and I'd help him. You know, I'd just throw out ideas, or whatever."

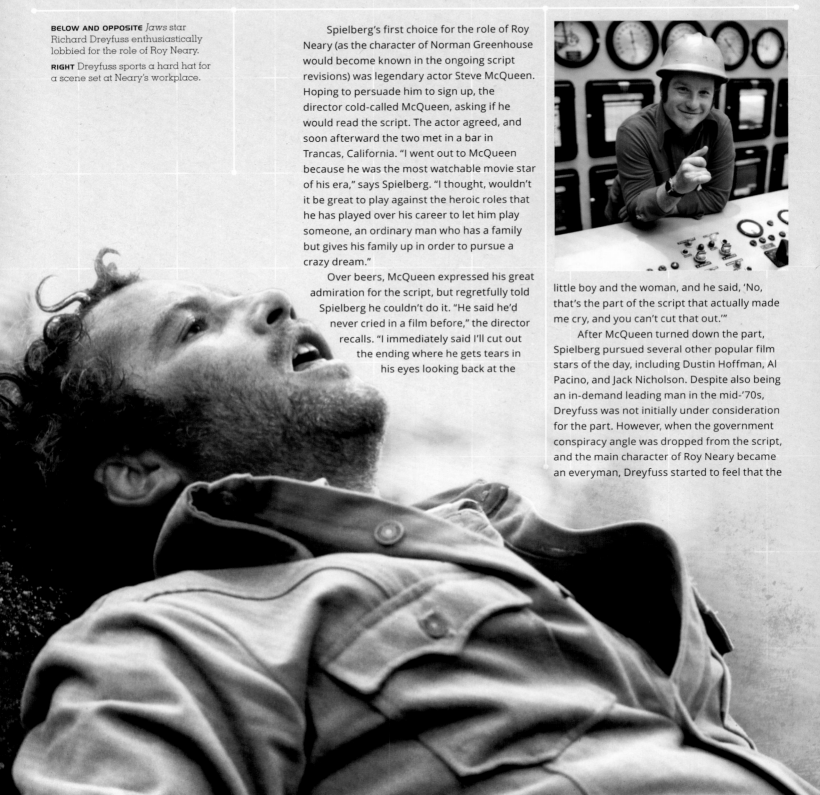

BELOW AND OPPOSITE *Jaws* star Richard Dreyfuss enthusiastically lobbied for the role of Roy Neary.

RIGHT Dreyfuss sports a hard hat for a scene set at Neary's workplace.

Spielberg's first choice for the role of Roy Neary (as the character of Norman Greenhouse would become known in the ongoing script revisions) was legendary actor Steve McQueen. Hoping to persuade him to sign up, the director cold-called McQueen, asking if he would read the script. The actor agreed, and soon afterward the two met in a bar in Trancas, California. "I went out to McQueen because he was the most watchable movie star of his era," says Spielberg. "I thought, wouldn't it be great to play against the heroic roles that he has played over his career to let him play someone, an ordinary man who has a family but gives his family up in order to pursue a crazy dream."

Over beers, McQueen expressed his great admiration for the script, but regretfully told Spielberg he couldn't do it. "He said he'd never cried in a film before," the director recalls. "I immediately said I'll cut out the ending where he gets tears in his eyes looking back at the little boy and the woman, and he said, 'No, that's the part of the script that actually made me cry, and you can't cut that out.'"

After McQueen turned down the part, Spielberg pursued several other popular film stars of the day, including Dustin Hoffman, Al Pacino, and Jack Nicholson. Despite also being an in-demand leading man in the mid-'70s, Dreyfuss was not initially under consideration for the part. However, when the government conspiracy angle was dropped from the script, and the main character of Roy Neary became an everyman, Dreyfuss started to feel that the

role was made for him. "I knew this was not about a lifer in the Army," he explains. "This was about someone who had to have a special quality. All of a sudden, I became overwhelmed with possession about this part. I set out, for the first and only time in my life, to bad-mouth every actor in Hollywood. I would walk by Steven's office and say things like 'Al Pacino has no sense of humor,' or 'Jack Nicholson's crazy,' or whatever I had to say."

Although he intended his comments to be something of a joke, Dreyfuss was adamant that Neary needed to be played by a regular actor, not a movie star. "When you're a movie star," he explains, "you're not common, and the audience has to suspend disbelief that Humphrey Bogart is common. This film could never have worked with Cary Grant, or Steve McQueen or any of those guys. I was a common man, and that's what was the strength of my career."

While Spielberg and Dreyfuss had bonded on *Jaws* and become friends, it was actually this closeness that initially made the director reluctant to cast the actor. "I saw a lot of myself in Richard," Spielberg explains. "I didn't want to cast myself as Neary in *Close Encounters*, and by casting Richard, I would be casting myself. I finally came back to the realization that *I*

wrote this. I'm on every page that Neary is. So why not go back to Richard, who was the first person I ever talked to about *Close Encounters*, and cast him, and, therefore, [infuse] a little bit of myself in the role?"

Dreyfuss recalls another insight that he believes was integral to Spielberg's decision to give him the role. "In order to pull this story off, you had to have a sense of wonder, which I knew I had, and Steven knew I had," he states. "I knew this character had to have the sense of a child. One day, I walked by his office, and I said, 'Steven, you need a child.' And he looked up and said, 'You got the part.'"

"One of the things Richard and I shared in common is that we've both been big kids all our lives," Spielberg notes.

For the actor, getting the part of Roy Neary was more than just a chance to work with his friend on another movie. He had been taken with the premise of *Close Encounters* from the very beginning, in particular the film's peaceful, reassuring message. "I knew the minute they started talking about this film that this was a noble idea," says Dreyfuss. "Just on its face, it's a film with a higher ambition, a higher reach than our ability to grasp. I knew that this would outlive us all."

35

THEY WERE INVITED

With Dreyfuss confirmed as Roy Neary, Spielberg turned his attention to filling out the rest of his ensemble cast.

OPPOSITE Comedienne/actress Teri Garr won the role of Ronnie Neary when Spielberg spotted her in a commercial.

ABOVE AND TOP Acclaimed director François Truffaut agreed to appear as UFO expert Claude Lacombe.

To play Roy's long-suffering wife, Ronnie, the director chose actress Teri Garr. Although Garr was an established actress with roles in dozens of television episodes and in such films as *Young Frankenstein* and *The Conversation*, it was the strength of her performance in a TV coffee commercial that won her the role. Spielberg was so taken with the housewife character Garr portrayed in the thirty-second ad that he knew he had found his Ronnie Neary.

Although Spielberg was sure Garr was right for Ronnie, in a 1997 documentary about the making of *Close Encounters*, the actress recalled that she had other ideas: "I told him [Spielberg] I wanted to play [Jillian Guiler]; it's a much better part. He said, 'No, no, I want you to play the wife.' I said no. Where I got this arrogance from, I have no idea."

Spielberg stuck to his guns, and Garr came around. "I had so many girlfriends at the time and relatives in my family that were married to men, and they just lived their lives through them, and they had a bunch of kids, and they ran the house, and they did all that stuff," she said. "I felt, I know who this woman is, and I'd

be up to it, and I'd like to try it. I was attracted to work with Steven Spielberg, just because he was a great filmmaker, and I knew this was going to be a big movie."

When Spielberg changed the nationality of Lacombe from American to French, his first choice for the role was François Truffaut, a fellow filmmaker of great international acclaim who had written and directed French New Wave classics like *The 400 Blows* (1959) and *Jules and Jim* (1962), and acted in a number of his own films. "I wanted this film to have global implications," says Spielberg. "I wanted the story to be bigger than a little piece of American mythology. I wanted it to really affect the entire world, so I thought that the head of the operation should be someone like François Truffaut, [specifically] the character he played in *The Wild Child*, which is why I thought of him."

Nervous that Truffaut, one of his cinematic idols—who, with the exception of appearances in a couple of friends' shorts, had never acted in a film other than his own—would turn him down, Spielberg traveled to France and met with other actors. "I met with Jean-Louis

37

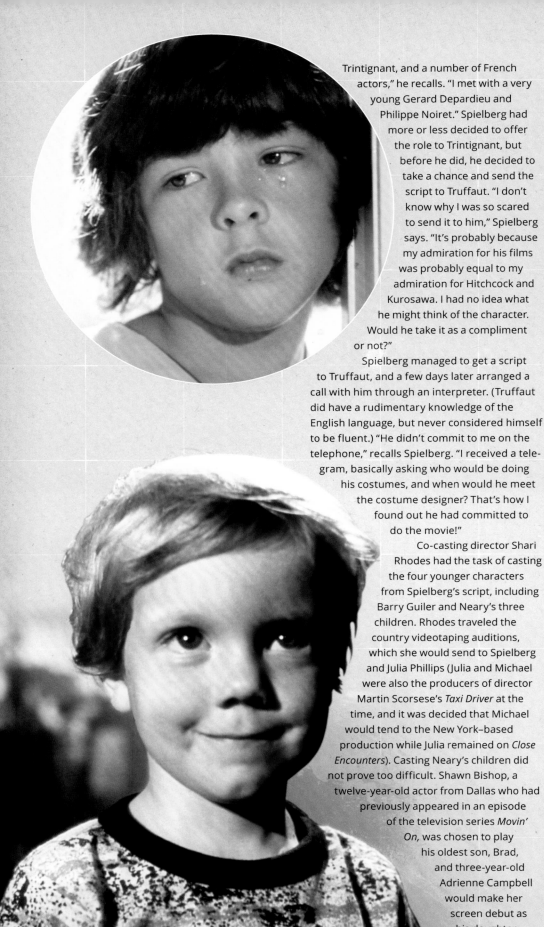

Trintignant, and a number of French actors," he recalls. "I met with a very young Gerard Depardieu and Philippe Noiret." Spielberg had more or less decided to offer the role to Trintignant, but before he did, he decided to take a chance and send the script to Truffaut. "I don't know why I was so scared to send it to him," Spielberg says. "It's probably because my admiration for his films was probably equal to my admiration for Hitchcock and Kurosawa. I had no idea what he might think of the character. Would he take it as a compliment or not?"

Spielberg managed to get a script to Truffaut, and a few days later arranged a call with him through an interpreter. (Truffaut did have a rudimentary knowledge of the English language, but never considered himself to be fluent.) "He didn't commit to me on the telephone," recalls Spielberg. "I received a telegram, basically asking who would be doing his costumes, and when would he meet the costume designer? That's how I found out he had committed to do the movie!"

Co-casting director Shari Rhodes had the task of casting the four younger characters from Spielberg's script, including Barry Guiler and Neary's three children. Rhodes traveled the country videotaping auditions, which she would send to Spielberg and Julia Phillips (Julia and Michael were also the producers of director Martin Scorsese's *Taxi Driver* at the time, and it was decided that Michael would tend to the New York–based production while Julia remained on *Close Encounters*). Casting Neary's children did not prove too difficult. Shawn Bishop, a twelve-year-old actor from Dallas who had previously appeared in an episode of the television series *Movin' On*, was chosen to play his oldest son, Brad, and three-year-old Adrienne Campbell would make her screen debut as his daughter,

Silvia. The third Neary child, eight-year-old Toby, was found when Richard Dreyfuss suggested to Spielberg that his nephew Justin could play the part. Young Justin Dreyfuss did bear a resemblance to his uncle and had the requisite acting ability, and so Spielberg added a second Dreyfuss to the cast.

Unfortunately, Rhodes wasn't having as much luck casting the key role of Barry Guiler. Having searched many a preschool to no avail, she finally came up with a strong candidate named Zack Bowman, and sent footage of him to Spielberg and Julia Phillips. Coincidently, while picking up her niece at a preschool in Atlanta, she spotted another likely candidate, three-year-old Cary Guffey, who she felt had a special quality that might work for Barry.

Speaking today, Guffey recalls that one of his very first vivid memories was overhearing his mother on the phone saying, "Not *the* Columbia Pictures??" in disbelief when the studio called to arrange a screen test. "It was a very unique thing to have happen," says Guffey. "It wasn't something we'd gone looking for. I was in a preschool class. The casting director walked in, saw me, and said, 'That's the kid!' It was just dumb luck."

Watching the screen tests of both Cary and Zack, Spielberg couldn't make a decision between the two boys. Since there would be at least six weeks of filming to be done before the character of Barry made his first screen appearance, the director decided he would bring them both to Mobile and do his own screen test on location.

TOP The Neary siblings, Brad, Silvia, and Toby: Shawn Bishop (top left), Adrienne Campbell (top), and Justin Dreyfuss (above).

LEFT Three-year-old Cary Guffey won the role of Barry Guiler.

OPPOSITE Spielberg with Cary Guffey.

THE FINAL PIECES

In further revisions of the script, Lacombe's interpreter lost what had been described as a "thick Brooklyn accent" and gained a name: David Laughlin. Co-casting director Juliet Taylor strongly recommended actor Bob Balaban for the role. Taylor had cast Balaban in two of his first films when the actor was still in his senior year of college: *Catch-22* and Best Picture Academy Award winner *Midnight Cowboy*. While on a trip to New York, Taylor set up a meeting for Balaban with Spielberg, Julia Phillips, and Richard Dreyfuss, who was a personal friend of the actor. "[Juliet] told me I was up for the part of an interpreter, I had to speak French," recalls Balaban. "I told her I spoke beautiful French. I had studied French in high school, and my accent was good, but it had been fifteen years since I'd had a French course, and I wasn't exactly fluent at that point!"

ABOVE Bob Balaban (left) as Lacombe's translator, David Laughlin.

OPPOSITE After an exhaustive search, Melinda Dillon was hired to play Jillian Guiler three days before the start of shooting.

BELOW Dillon and Spielberg confer on set.

Spielberg explained to Balaban that the role involved translating from French to English and vice versa, and that they were hoping he was going to be working directly with François Truffaut, although, at the time of Balaban's casting, the French actor hadn't yet officially agreed to take on the role. "I first explained in French that it had been many years since I'd spoken French, and if they gave me the job, it was going to be very difficult for me," says Balaban. "So I wasn't lying, but I was speaking very nice French because I had looked up every word, and written it down and memorized it, so it seemed to them that I was speaking conversationally, and they had no idea what I was saying, because nobody in the room spoke French. And then after a little bit, they asked if I could say a few more words, and I recited a poem called 'The Ants and the Grasshopper,' about how industrious the ant is, and how much the grasshopper never saves for the winter. They thought my French was great."

Balaban was hired on the spot. "I ran out to Berlitz [Language Learning Center] the next day and really started trying to learn French," he says.

Although Balaban seemed to have the job in the bag, there was one stipulation from Spielberg: The actor was required to keep the beard he sported during the audition. Unfortunately, he was about to appear in a stage version of *Catch-22* where he needed to be clean-shaven. "I was supposed to be in the Army, and I wouldn't have been allowed to have a beard," says Balaban. "I kept a kind of low growth going during the entire play so that by the time the movie started, my beard would be sort of up to beard par."

While the beard clause seemed bizarre to Balaban at first, there was sound reasoning behind the request. He and Dreyfuss were similar in terms of look, build, and age, and Spielberg wanted to make sure that there was a clear visual delineation between them onscreen. "Steven said it was important that people not confuse Richard Dreyfuss and me when they saw the movie," Balaban explains. "Richard had gotten really, really famous because of *Jaws*, in which he wore wireframe glasses and had a beard. Richard was going to shave his beard, and *not* wear glasses in *Close Encounters*, and so Steven decided that I would wear wireframe glasses and a beard [to differentiate us]."

By far, the biggest casting challenge turned out to be finding an actress to play Jillian Guiler. The team had met with a number of prospects, but the actresses either couldn't do the film, or weren't deemed right for the role. Three days before the start of production, they still hadn't found their Jillian. The first day of filming would feature the character, and Spielberg was on the verge of having to majorly rework the shooting schedule when director Hal Ashby contacted him with a suggestion. Ashby had been filming *Bound for Glory*, a Woody Guthrie biopic that starred David Carradine as the legendary folk singer and Melinda Dillon as his wife.

"I think [Ashby] probably found out from the agencies who were clamoring to put their clients in my movie, or maybe found out through his agent," says Spielberg. "I was a tremendous fan of Hal. I had met him twice previously, and he called me out of the blue and said he heard I was looking for a lead actress to be in my film, and would I like to see a couple of reels of *Bound for Glory*. I went to his place, and I got to see Melinda in a few scenes. She was perfect."

Having just wrapped the film with Ashby, Dillon suddenly found herself bound for Los Angeles to meet with Spielberg. Before the meeting, however, she didn't read the *Close Encounters* script the production had sent her.

"It was a space movie, which was something I wasn't interested in at all," she explains. "I kind of flipped through the thing, looking for Jillian, and then I found it. 'And she's taking the most exciting photographs ever taken in the world.' For a moment, I saw what that would be like, to be taking pictures of these creatures. And I got very excited, just with that image. I thought, 'Okay, I'll go in and meet with these people, but I probably won't do it.'"

At Spielberg's LA office, Dillon, a Tony-nominated veteran of the Broadway stage, felt like a fish out of water. "Steven and Julia Phillips and the costume designer were there, and other people roaming around in Steven's office," she remembers. "And Steven was going, 'Aren't you excited? I want you for my movie!' All of them were young, enthusiastic, and nothing like Broadway . . . But when [Spielberg] told me Hal pieced together some

of the scenes from [*Bound for Glory*], and he knew I had to be Jillian, I thought, 'Well, if from that role he sees me in this, then it's not just one of these sci-fi things that I can't stand. It's got to be something else.'" Dillon accepted the part, and within twenty-four hours was on her way to the shooting location.

Needless to say, Spielberg was hugely relieved to have found his Jillian Guiler just in the nick of time. "We started shooting on Monday, and I found her on the Wednesday before!" says the director.

Other actors who were cast included Lance Henriksen as Robert, Lacombe's driver; Warren J. Kemmerling as Major "Wild Bill" Walsh; Roberts Blossom as the quirky farmer who Roy meets at Crescendo Summit; Josef Sommer as Larry Butler, who escapes from the Army helicopter with Roy and Jillian; and George DiCenzo as Air Force debunker Major Benchley.

CHOICES

Between the months of February and May of 1976, a great number of elements needed to be finalized. The film was scheduled to begin shooting on May 17 in Wyoming, where the Devils Tower exteriors would be shot. (The crew would be based in the town of Gillette, just over sixty miles from the landmark.) The time spent in Wyoming would give Joe Alves the opportunity to complete the giant Box Canyon set at Brookley Air Force Base in Alabama, where the production would be based for the remainder of filming. The only remaining scene not to be shot in Alabama, a sequence where Lacombe and Laughlin visit a village in India, was scheduled to be filmed in Bombay (now known as Mumbai) after completion of the main shoot.

A watertight schedule was, of course, crucial to successfully shooting a film as complicated as *Close Encounters*. When creating a master schedule for the film, first assistant director Chuck Myers and his second AD, Jim Bloom, pored over the script, planning each day meticulously, from the number of extras needed to what equipment would be required on set. When they were done, they found that the eighty-five days of shooting that Columbia Pictures had signed off on would not be enough. They needed two more days. Unable to decide which two days to snip out of the schedule, they

took the matter to Spielberg. The film's schedule was laid out on a big accordion-like board, into which thin cardboard strips, representing specific days and scenes, were inserted. "We walked in, and I remember Chuck saying to Steven, 'Well, I'm kind of stumped,'" recalls Bloom. "'I don't know where to take it [the two days] from' . . . Steven picked up the board and shook it physically, and two days fell out. He said, 'There are your two days. Let's go!'"

Before shooting could begin, the production needed to decide which film format would be used for the all-important visual

effects scenes. The wrong choice could mean producing scenes that lacked the sense of awe Spielberg was determined to achieve. Trumbull had, from the beginning, lobbied for the 70mm process, which had been used for *2001: A Space Odyssey*. "Whenever you're doing visual effects, every time you duplicate the negative in order to add [a visual effect], you get a buildup of grain and contrast, and it lowers the quality of the image," he says. "Even though the bulk of [*Close Encounters* would be] shot in 35mm anamorphic, all of the visual effects were shot in 65mm, so that by the time it was duplicated, it would be still as good in quality as the original 35mm material." The extra 5 millimeters was taken up by the informational data that would accommodate the soundtrack, thereby making the film's width 70mm in total.

Both Spielberg and the studio agreed that 70mm was the best option. However, Trumbull knew that in order to fully realize Spielberg's vision for the visual effects sequences, he would have to push beyond the limits of existing visual effects technology. At the time, visual effects scenes that were added to live-action footage required that the camera capturing the action on set be stationary. During filming, a certain portion of the frame would be designated for the visual effect that would be added in postproduction, and no on-set elements, be they actors or props, would be able to enter or block that section of the frame for fear of spoiling the final visual effect. These "lock-off" shots would not work for Spielberg on *Close Encounters*, however, as he wanted his UFOs to interact with locations and characters in a dynamic and believable way. To achieve this organic quality, the camera needed to be able to move. Some of the film's shots would also require the combination of a number of special effects disciplines, including matte paintings, miniatures, and animation, and in order to seamlessly blend all these elements with the live action, they would need a system that was perfectly precise.

"We proposed the idea of developing a [computerized] motion control system so that we could digitally record the camera's motion . . . whenever we went on location, and then be able to play that camera motion back into a miniature camera system for adding UFOs or the Mothership or other extraneous stuff," says Trumbull. "Steven supported that, and we engaged a team of engineers to start building the control system for the film, which was a really big breakthrough."

Trumbull's computer-based motion control system would give his visual effects team all the data they needed to perfectly replicate the camera moves from the live-action scenes when combining that footage with miniature shots and other visual effects elements, preventing any overlapping of the various components that could ruin the scenes.

"We would record the precise movements of the dolly, and the pan and the tilt of the camera itself, and then the computer would play that tape back," Spielberg says. "The camera would then be slave to a computer, and the camera would be able to make subsequent passes on the other effects being created in postproduction that would then be layered over the original live-action plate." George

Lucas had used a similar system for *Star Wars* (Trumbull's father, Don, built the hardware for it), but the difference was that Lucas had used it only for scenes involving spaceships and other models. Trumbull's motion control system was the first to successfully blend non-static live-action footage of actors on set with visual effects, achieving stunning results.

Lighting would also be a crucial element in *Close Encounters*, in terms of capturing the sense of visual wonder Spielberg was looking for on set, and in the way in which the studio lights would interplay with the visual effects. Vilmos Zsigmond was very much a proponent of using natural light whenever possible and had even suggested shooting the film documentary-style, a notion Spielberg considered but ultimately decided not to pursue.

Regardless of his overall approach, one of the biggest challenges Zsigmond would face on the film would be lighting the Box Canyon set. To plan the sequence, the cinematographer began by studying the scale model that Joe Alves had built. Wanting to explore whether the banks of football stadium–style lights that Alves had included in his model would be sufficient to light the actual set, Zsigmond joined Alves on a trip to Pasadena's Rose Bowl, where, with a roll of tape, the production designer outlined the dimensions of his proposed set on the stadium grounds, and then had the lights turned on to their brightest. With a light meter in hand, Zsigmond took readings from all angles of the stadium, until he was convinced that a similar setup would work for him in Alabama.

OPPOSITE Spielberg directs a scene.

TOP Cinematographer Vilmos Zsigmond on the set of *Close Encounters*.

ABOVE Douglas Trumbull demonstrates a special effects shot for his director.

THE FIVE NOTES

Normally, a film composer doesn't start work on a score until after shooting has been completed and the first cut has been assembled. In the case of *Close Encounters*, John Williams was called upon to provide two key pieces of music at the start of filming that would play a key role in the shoot itself.

The idea that mankind and the alien visitors would communicate via music had been a part of Spielberg's story from the start. "There was no mode of thought leading up to that," the director explains. "It just seemed like the most perfect communion between them and us. When I was finished with the script, I took it to John Williams, and he said, 'This makes complete mathematical sense to me.'"

Williams was intrigued by the notion and was aware that the idea of communication through music had some historical basis. The composer explains that both Hungarian composer Zoltán Kodály and Russian composer Alexander Scriabin had "ideas that musical notes might have color. That a G would be red and an A would be pink and so on, and that messages could be sent back and forth in this way, and connected to sign language as well."

The first piece he was tasked to create was the "Five Notes," the auspicious opening of communication between earthlings and the visitors. "Steven asked me to write a five-note

RIGHT AND BELOW George Jensen production illustrations of the giant light board and ARP synthesizer used to communicate with the aliens.

OPPOSITE BOTTOM LEFT A page from the musical score for John Williams's iconic piece "The Dialogue."

combination of tones," says Williams. "I found it difficult because I kept saying to him, 'Seven notes is a melody, and three notes is just for the doorbell ring, and five notes is somewhere in between.'"

Spielberg was resolute in his decision. "I don't know why I knew it had be five tones," he says. "I just knew that seven was a song, and five was a suggestion. That, for me, five tones opens up, invites a conversation. And seven tones *is* a conversation."

With Spielberg's directive in mind, Williams wrote several hundred combinations of notes that they would both review daily. "We both kept circling this one, for no logical or explainable reason," says Williams. "So it was the result purely of a random search for something that we were looking for: *re, mi, do, do, sol*."

For the scenes that would follow the initial contact with the aliens, Williams continued the conversation with "The Dialogue," a compilation of various notes that, as the name of the piece suggests, would form a prolonged tonal exchange with the Mothership. To create this piece, Williams employed the theory of aleatoric music, loosely defined as music in which chance or indeterminate elements are left for the performer, or composer, to improvise. "'Any note can follow any other note,'" explains Williams, citing poet Ezra Pound.

Ultimately, when composing "The Dialogue," Williams's work would be informed by the extraterrestrial audience to whom it was directed. "I can only say that it was a random selection of things meant to sound random to us, that might be intelligible to another creature," he says.

Both of Williams's compositions were recorded in Burbank to be played back during the shooting of the scenes.

LAST WRITES?

The script of *Close Encounters* remained a work in progress throughout the preproduction process and even into the shoot. If there was a scene that troubled Spielberg or if he suddenly hit upon a great new idea, he wouldn't hesitate to make revisions to the screenplay, sometimes recruiting his writer friends to help. On a New York casting trip in February 1976, Spielberg had called upon one of those friends, screenwriter and producer Jerry Belson, to give him an outside perspective on the ever-evolving script. Belson traveled to the Big Apple, where together they worked on adding even more depth and dimension to some of the film's characters. "I brought him in and we wrote together for three weeks," Spielberg says. "[He] sprinkled the script with much-needed humor, and he really made a big contribution to the movie." It was during this time with Belson that Norman Greenhouse became Roy Neary and the international UFO tracking group was first dubbed the Mayflower Project, among many other changes.

As more scenes were added, others were dropped from the script. The discovery of the SS *Marine Sulphur Queen* in the Gobi Desert and the five World War II Navy planes in the jungles of Brazil were both deemed cost prohibitive. The scene where the Air Force major debunks Roy's claims remained, but the aftermath, in which Neary rewired the building lights to spell out "UFO," was lost. The group of people assembled at Crescendo Summit were no longer dubbed the Society for the People Interested in What's Going On Around Here, and Jillian no longer discussed her previous encounters.

In March, approximately six weeks before he was to begin shooting, Spielberg invited writers Matthew Robbins and Hal Barwood to give the script a final polish. Since Spielberg first approached them, the writing duo's sci-fi project had been shelved, so they were now available to offer their suggestions. Much of their work involved tweaks to already established scenes, such as expanding a sequence where Roy rips up his yard to gather the materials for building an enormous model of Devils Tower in his living room. His meeting with the government representative at the Air Force base, which started as a one-on-one, now became a "town hall" gathering, in which Roy was joined by many of the people he had met at Crescendo Summit.

With only a few days left before shooting, Robbins and Barwood delivered their most important contribution, a significant plot development that would have major implications for the shooting schedule. In previous drafts, Jillian Guiler's narrative arc did little more than mirror Roy's story. In order to up the dramatic stakes and flesh out Jillian's character, the writing duo added a plotline in which the extraterrestrials abduct her son, Barry, from their home, with the frantic Jillian traveling to Devils Tower to try to find her missing child.

"CLOSE ENCOUNTERS OF THE THIRD KIND"

by

Steven Spielberg

REVISED:
March 1st, 1976
(SS changes included)

Property of:
PHILLIPS PRODUCTIONS
4000 Warner Blvd.
Burbank, California 91505
(213) 843-6000 Ext.: 1736

ROUGH TYPE

*Ronnie should say—
"You've been fired!
Let her just say it*

JILL RUNS INTO KITCHEN AS BARRY OPENS KITCHEN DOOR.

AS JILLIAN SLAMS KITCHEN DOOR, LIL' BARRY HEADS BACK TOWARD DINING ROOM.

ABOVE The cover page of Spielberg's penultimate draft of the *Close Encounters* screenplay.

RIGHT George Jensen storyboards show the arrival of the aliens at the Guiler home, and Jillian's frantic attempts to protect Barry.

OPPOSITE TOP RIGHT Spielberg and producer Julia Phillips sit on the tarmac as the crew prepare a passenger plane for filming.

PAGES 48–49 Military personnel watch the stars come to life and head for Box Canyon in George Jensen's preproduction artwork.

JILLIAN DUCKS UNDER TABLE. APPLIANCES START UP (VARIOUS INSERTS)

JILLIAN FREAKING OUT BARRY DELIGHTED

TELEPHONE OPERATORS VOICE ON TAPE ..."PLEASE CHECK NUMBER & DIAL AGAIN."

ANGLE FROM UNDER TABLE. DISHWASHER TURNS ON

Spielberg loved the idea, but it became a serious matter of contention with Columbia Pictures, which received the revision when Spielberg was already in Wyoming getting ready to begin shooting. It wasn't the content of the scene that irked the executives, but the fact that they had not been consulted about the change—not to mention that the revisions would add shooting days to the schedule and, therefore, cost to the budget. "Up until then, there had been a collaboration in the sense that nothing was a great big surprise to us," recounts Stanley Jaffe. "All of a sudden, this popped up when they had [already] left to shoot." David Begelman sent Jaffe to the Wyoming location to express their extreme displeasure with this turn of events. "My going out there was not something they were looking forward to, because they knew it was going to lead to a discussion about what was angering us," Jaffe adds. "I know Julia was not happy, and she wasn't an easy person to deal with. She protected Steven like a mother [protecting her] cub."

Indeed, when Julia Phillips heard that Jaffe was on his way, she quickly formulated a plan that would counter any threats to shut down

the production. "Julia [had] said to me, 'Pack your bags, we're leaving,'" recalls Spielberg. "'We're telling Stanley we quit. Unless you can make your movie, there's no reason we should continue with this project,' and I agreed with her. We brought our luggage to the restaurant where we were meeting him. She had many more bags than I did. I remember that. The bags, I think, spoke louder than anything we could have said in rebuttal." Ultimately, the storm passed, the new plot development remained, and Jaffe even stayed in Wyoming to witness the first day of shooting.

Throughout the production, Spielberg would have a congenial relationship with the executives at Columbia Pictures (aided by Julia Phillips's shielding), but before he left to begin production, the studio made it very clear that they were expecting him to deliver nothing less than a *Jaws*-size hit. "They pretty much said that to me from the get-go," he confirms. "'This is blockbuster or bust time.' That's something I would never tell one of our directors at DreamWorks or Amblin Partners. I had that sword of Damocles over my head every second of production."

PART TWO

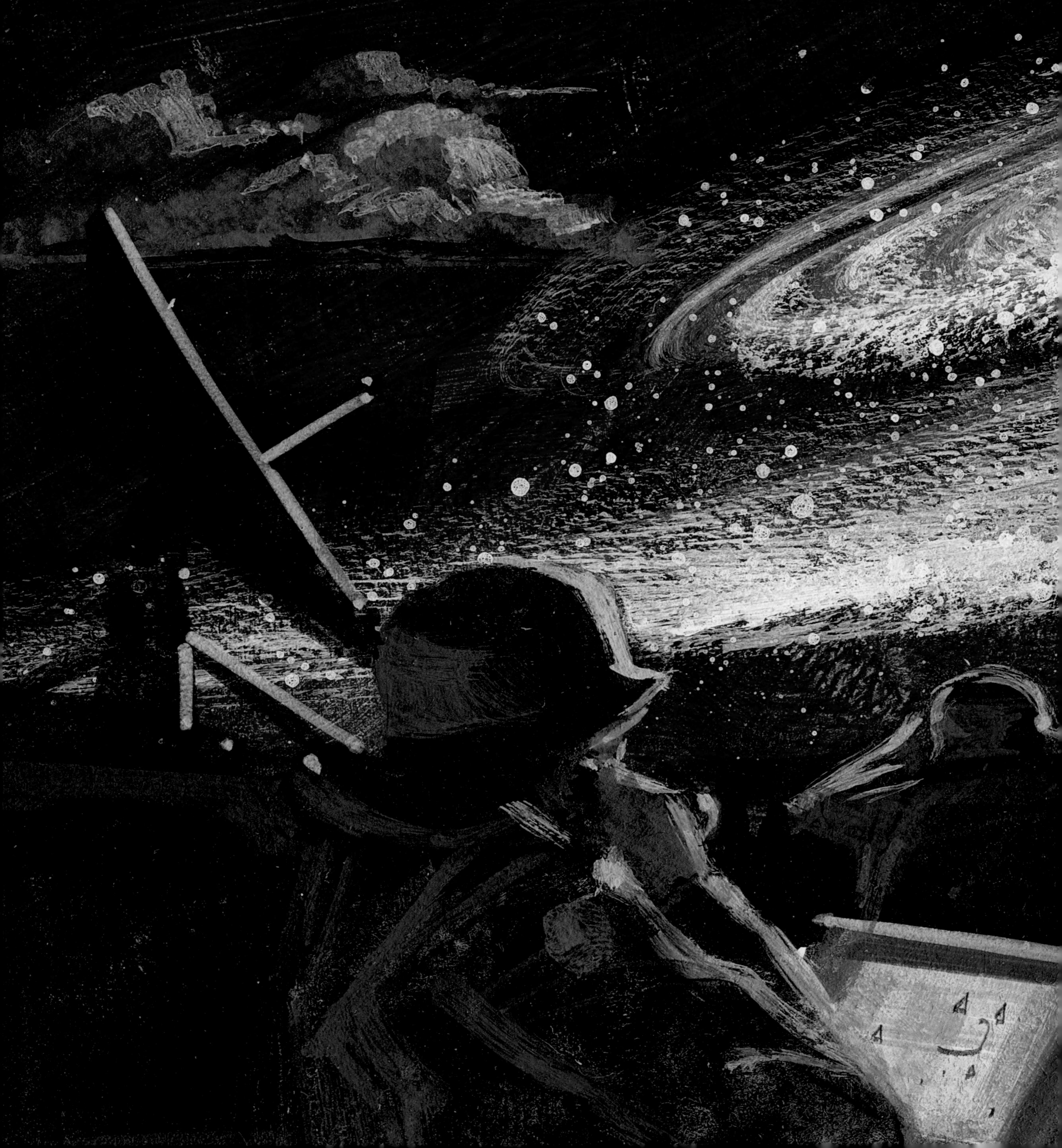

DEVILS TOWER (MAY 17–28, 1976)

Close Encounters of the Third Kind began principal photography on location in Wyoming on Monday, May 17, 1976. The first shot captured would be from the scene where Roy reaches the outskirts of Reliance, Wyoming—in real life approximately four hundred miles from Devils Tower—and drives past the refugees being evacuated by the government. It was an ambitious sequence featuring over two hundred extras, laden with luggage, and dozens of vehicles, both civilian and military.

Once the refugee scene was complete, Spielberg hunched down in the back of a station wagon to give direction to Richard Dreyfuss and Melinda Dillon as they performed the scene where Roy and Jillian drive toward Devils Tower on the final leg of their journey. For Dillon, being confined to a car for the sequence was a godsend because, unbeknownst to anyone in production, right after being cast by Spielberg, she had a mishap in her LA hotel that left her with a broken toe. "My foot swelled, and it turned black and it was horrible to walk," she says. "I thought 'Uh-oh. There goes that job.' I taped it up real tight, and then we had to get on the plane and go to Wyoming. For days and

days I was hiding the fact that I had a broken toe. Nobody was ever told."

Bob Balaban had his own dilemma. Originally not scheduled to work until the end of the first week of shooting, the actor suddenly got a call from production telling him he needed to be on location for that first day. Because bad weather had been forecast, the production had to be prepared to switch from shooting the Devils Tower exteriors to shooting interiors at the location instead, all of which required Balaban's character. If he wasn't there, the company would have precious little to shoot and come to a standstill on the very first day. The problem was that when the

ABOVE Spielberg crams into the back of a station wagon to direct Dreyfuss and Dillon in the very first scenes to be filmed in Wyoming.

BELOW The crew lines the highway to film the evacuation of the population of Reliance, Wyoming.

OPPOSITE The crew are dwarfed by the full majesty of Devils Tower.

actor received the call he was still appearing onstage in *Catch-22* in Stamford, Connecticut, "My closing performance happened literally the day before the first shooting date," says Balaban. A limousine waited for him outside the theater, and when the curtain came down, the actor began a fourteen-hour journey to reach the set. "There was some red-eye that got me vaguely close to Wyoming, and then I had to take another plane that took me to Jackson Hole," he recalls. "And then I had to take something smaller that took me nearer to Gillette." When a weary Balaban finally arrived, he discovered that the weather was perfect, which meant that he wouldn't be needed for another several days. "But, it gave me a little time for my beard to grow longer!" he says.

The free time also gave Balaban an opportunity to get acquainted with François Truffaut over dinner, although the local Gillette cuisine proved a little baffling to the French auteur. "We went out to a modest sort of buffet restaurant, and the first thing I had to do was to explain to François what chicken-fried steak was," says Balaban. "It is impossible to translate chicken-fried steak into meaningful French."

Because the Devils Tower location was a long, bumpy, hour-long drive away from

the motel where most of the cast and crew were being housed, for the sake of time and convenience, Spielberg and Dreyfuss were provided with mobile homes just minutes away from the location. François Truffaut was also offered a trailer, but declined, preferring the amenities of the Gillette motel.

Meanwhile, shooting continued on the scenes of Dreyfuss and Dillon heading for Devils Tower, including the moment where Roy and Jillian see various farm animals that have been downed by an apparent nerve gas leak. To achieve this moment, a team of veterinarians gave the animals a sedative minutes before the cameras were ready to roll. "I remember they knocked them out, and stood by," says second assistant director Jim Bloom. "Then [the animals] woke up and wandered away. No animals were harmed on this project."

In preparing the area where Spielberg would film Roy and Jillian's arrival at the entrance to Devils Tower, Joe Alves found himself on the receiving end of some unsolicited feedback from a local expert. The production designer had been constructing fencing with sections of logs strung together using barbed wire when a rancher approached

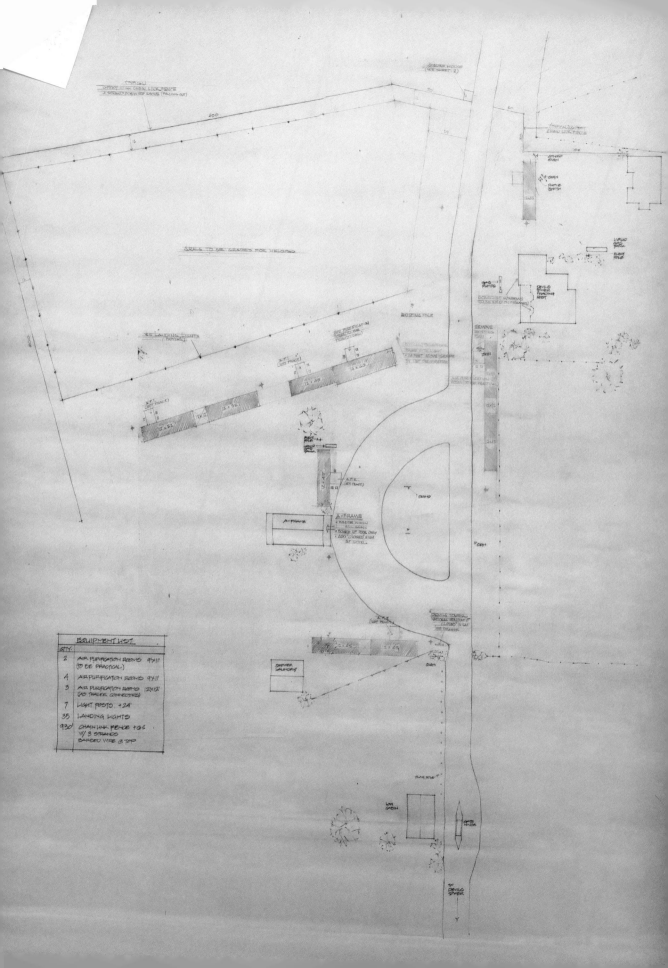

close down the park. "I said, 'No, we're not closing the park. We're just shooting [this sign that says] the park is closed,'" recalls Alves. "His response was 'No, you can't close the park. You have a sign that says "Park Closed."' This went back and forth a number of times. I could not convince him that I wasn't closing the park. I had to take it down."

One of the most complex elements of the Devils Tower shoot was the construction of the base camp/government complex at the foot of the butte itself. In preproduction, Spielberg, trying to be mindful of the ever-growing budget, gave Alves a ballpark figure of $5,000 for the set, a number that would later prove to be overly optimistic. "I needed a facility, trailers, helicopters, lots of stuff," Alves says. "I went to [line producer] Clark [Paylow], and he said, 'What do you have figured for it?' I said 'about fifty [$50,000].' He said, 'Just do what you have to do. I'll take care of it.'" Alves got the $50,000 he needed, but he also saved a few dollars by featuring the trucks that hauled the production's equipment in the film itself, dressing them as the government haulers that are camouflaged with the brand logos of popular businesses of the day, including Baskin-Robbins and Piggly Wiggly.

After being on hold, François Truffaut and Bob Balaban finally began work on May 20, four days into filming. Their first scene required

OPPOSITE TOP Dreyfuss, Dillon, Spielberg, and the crew prepare for a shot on a Devils Tower overlook.

OPPOSITE BOTTOM In a scene deleted from the final film, Neary tries to convince the occupants of a military helicopter that he's not a looter and is paying for the gas he's taking.

ABOVE Spielberg and Zsigmond frame the reveal of Devils Tower.

BELOW The on-location Army facility and containment area set (right side of image) sits across the road from the production base camp.

him and made it clear that these were not the kind of fences they used in Wyoming. "They had certain traditions and laws and rules, and they didn't like the fence I was putting up," says Alves. He explained to the rancher that immediately after they filmed the scene, the offending fences would be taken down.

Alves also ran into trouble over another piece of set dressing related to the military shutdown scenes: a sign erected at the main entrance to Devils Tower announcing that the park was closed. On seeing the sign, a park official confronted Alves, informing him that the production did not have the authority to

them to follow Richard Dreyfuss as he was led to the helicopter filled with the other people who have been compelled to travel to Devils Tower. Balaban and Truffaut were grateful to not have any dialogue in the scene, giving them a chance to ease into the production and get a sense of the tone Spielberg was trying to set. During filming of the sequence, Spielberg's instincts on Balaban's beard proved correct when an extra approached Balaban and, thinking he was Dreyfuss, began asking him questions about the shark in *Jaws*. Balaban gamely told the extra that the shark had very big teeth.

One of the few interior scenes shot at the Devils Tower location took place in a small Quonset hut built by the production on site, where Lacombe, aided by his translator, Laughlin, tries to convince Wild Bill, the military commander of the operation, to allow Neary and the other visionaries to be allowed to participate in the classified event. Balaban recalls that the temperature in the cramped

set, filled with bodies, cameras and lights, rose to over 100 degrees. Adding to the uncomfortable environment was Truffaut's nervousness about the scene, which would require him to deliver the most dialogue since his arrival in Wyoming. To help remember his English dialogue, Truffaut wrote the lines on manila envelopes and taped them everywhere—the walls, the camera, and even on actor Warren J. Kemmerling's chest.

At 4 p.m. each day during the Devils Tower shoot, the production would quickly shift from whatever scene they were filming and move to the base of the tower to capture the scenes of Roy, Jillian, and Larry making their way up into the surrounding forest to climb the mountain. In the context of the story, the scene began in late afternoon daylight (hence the 4 p.m. starting time), but as the trio made their way up the mountain, the sun would begin to set, with the action extending into the dark of night as they got close to the mountaintop.

OPPOSITE TOP The crew films Roy, Jillian, and Larry's attempt to reach the top of Devils Tower.

OPPOSITE BOTTOM As Bob Balaban and Lance Henriksen look on, Truffaut and Spielberg discuss an upcoming scene.

TOP AND ABOVE Vilmos Zsigmond supervises the preparation for a complicated camera move that will follow Richard Dreyfuss as he boards a helicopter.

The last few days of the sequence turned into full night shooting, with more than sixty crew members lugging equipment and having to navigate their way up and down the treacherous mountain paths. The paths were steep, and they had to travel a great distance from setup to setup, so the crew would carry only the bare minimum they would need to shoot, but this still amounted to hundreds of pounds of equipment.

"We would go up the rocks with the crew, and then it would get too dark, and we'd go down," remembers Dreyfuss. "We kept going further and further up, until one day, and it had escaped us all—Steven, Melinda, myself—that we were going farther and farther up as the sun was going lower and lower. And in a second, we all realized, 'Oops!' and we were in total darkness, and we were three quarters of the way up the rocks. There was no way we could move. It took two guys two hours to feel their way down to the road [to find lights and come back and rescue us]. Two hours in black darkness, with Steven and I telling each other stories to keep one another awake and laughing."

As a result of this mishap, lights became part of the essential equipment that the crew was required to carry for the rest of the time they spent on the mountain.

When shooting the moment where the trio make their break from the helicopter to start their escape up the mountain, Melinda Dillon managed to pick up a second injury. "They wanted to get a shot of us jumping out of the helicopter, and running and taking off," says the actress, who still hadn't told the production about her broken toe. Although the helicopter did have steps to make it easier to get in and out, when the camera rolled, and Spielberg yelled "Jump!," Dillon took him literally. "I looked down, and I thought, okay," she says. "And I jumped, and tore a muscle in my left thigh." As with her damaged toe, Dillon managed to soldier on, still worried that the company might replace her if they found out.

Fortunately, Dillon's situation improved greatly after a somewhat contentious car ride to the motel with François Truffaut. "I got carsick, and he was smoking these cigars in the car," she recalls. "Somebody told him, 'You're making Melinda sick . . . Could you please just wait?' He said, 'No. I've been working all day, and I'm going to smoke my cigars!'" However, the next day, to make amends, Truffaut offered Dillon use of the mobile home that he had turned down, which was situated next to the trailers of Spielberg and Dreyfuss. "I said yes immediately," exclaims Dillon. "I got to stay in that beautiful trailer, and the rain would come every night, and it was wonderful." Besides allowing her to bond with her director and leading man, staying in the mobile home gave Dillon a little more time to nurse her mounting injuries.

55

Transportation woes of a different type affected Truffaut during a scene shot at Devils Tower in which Lacombe and Laughlin climb into a helicopter to be flown to the far side of the mountain. Truffaut and Balaban were told that the aircraft would rise just a few feet into the air and then land. When the helicopter kept climbing higher and higher, both actors hastily grabbed for their seat belts, and fumbled around trying to get them buckled. "We were about two hundred feet in the air, and as the helicopter banked steeply to the left, the door flew open," recalls Balaban. "An extra rushed over, grabbed the door, slammed it, and the rest of us held on like crazy." Ultimately, despite the momentary terror they had endured, the scene would not be used in the film.

Spielberg admits that, in the first few days of shooting, he was a little intimidated by the prospect of directing one of his idols, but it didn't take long for Truffaut to put him at ease. "He was such a collaborator," Spielberg says. "There was something so open about Truffaut, and curious about him. He asked tons of questions, and not even about the movie we were making—just tons of questions about life.

We had wonderful conversations together, and I just found him to be a great companion to have on this journey."

Truffaut also developed a fondness for Spielberg during the shoot , although he did confide in Bob Balaban that he was somewhat nervous about acting in someone else's film, especially one in which he was required to speak English. There were several occasions when he asked Spielberg if he could deliver his lines in French and have Balaban provide the translation; however, for the most part the director would gently nudge him toward performing in English, and the actor would do his best to deliver. Conversely, on one or two occasions Truffaut delivered a line in English but with an accent so strong that Spielberg thought he was still speaking French!

Their work in Wyoming done, most of the cast and crew packed up and headed for Mobile, Alabama, just as tourists arrived at Devils Tower at the end of May for Memorial Day weekend. There were a few shots around Devils Tower that Spielberg still needed that didn't require the presence of actors, and since Douglas Trumbull also had some effects shots

ABOVE (left to right) Columbia Pictures head of production Stanley Jaffe, Spielberg, Phillips, and cast member Merrill Connally.

OPPOSITE TOP LEFT The name tag on Truffaut's dressing room at the Devils Tower location.

OPPOSITE TOP RIGHT Spielberg and Truffaut overcome the language barrier in between shots.

OPPOSITE BOTTOM Spielberg finds a rare moment to relax during the Wyoming shooting.

to complete, he and his director of photography for the photographic effects, Richard Yuricich, stayed behind to "mop up." Along with capturing the additional shots Spielberg required, the duo did some important groundwork for the visual effects marathon they would face in postproduction.

"We studied Devils Tower intimately and photographed it from every angle and started preparing how we were going to make that transition [from the exterior of Devils Tower to the interior set of the landing site] and [how] we were going to build miniatures of Devils Tower," Trumbull says. "We were going to use certain helicopter shots and things to link the two worlds together."

MOBILE, ALABAMA (MAY 29–SEPTEMBER 2, 1976)

The first scene to be filmed in Mobile was shot at a Holiday Inn, approximately twenty miles from the Holiday Inn in which the cast and crew were staying. The branch used for shooting was chosen because its exterior was less Southern-looking than others', a constant concern when choosing locations for a film that takes place in the Midwest, not the Deep South. In the scene itself—which was ultimately cut from the film—Laughlin receives word that the plans to meet the Mothership have been finalized and then rushes off to tell Lacombe. The scene required dozens of extras, playing members of the scientific team, to be sent back and forth around the motel's swimming pool, much to the chagrin of the paying guests, who were denied access to its cooling waters on a sweltering Alabama Saturday. At the end of the shooting day, both Truffaut and Balaban departed for several weeks of hiatus. Their characters would not be needed until the crew was ready to move into what everyone was referring to as the "Big Set"—the dirigible hangar at Brookley Air Force Base.

The crew went into full night mode during their first full week in Mobile to capture Roy Neary's first encounter with a UFO. Sent out by his employers to locate the source of the power outage in the area, Neary finds himself hopelessly lost and eventually pulls up to a railroad crossing, where he tries to find his location on a map. What seem to be the glaring headlights of a car appear behind Neary's truck, but the lights then rise over the vehicle, revealing to the audience, but not to Neary, that he is in the presence of a UFO. To achieve the effect, an arrangement of glaring lights (white, orange, and blue) was mounted on a crane and raised slowly out of camera frame, creating the illusion that the object in Roy's rearview mirror was flying over the car.

The next segment of the scene, when the presence of the UFO unleashes mayhem in and around Neary's truck, required a number of physical special effects from Roy Arbogast's team. Having already laid down ground fog around the area for atmosphere, they brought in a bank of old-fashioned mailboxes and a stop sign, all rigged with pneumatic devices that would cause the props to rattle and shake at the touch of a button. The real-life train crossing they had chosen for the shoot had no warning lights on either side of the track, so Arbogast brought his own, which had also been rigged

to rattle and shake, and had been fitted with lights that could manically flash on command. The piercing sounds of the warning bells would be added later, in postproduction. To create the high-intensity beam of light from the UFO that engulfs the truck, a special rig was constructed to hang several HMI lights over the vehicle. A fairly new piece of equipment at the time, but standard issue in the industry today, the HMIs (Hydrargyrum medium-arc iodine lamps) were powerful enough when combined to deliver a suitably intense beam.

Because the tracks were fully active and used by freight trains throughout the night, for safety reasons the AD staff had to be in constant communication with the local railroad authorities. Not only did the production team have to constantly reference the freight train schedule for the area, but a railroad company representative would also call the production well in advance of each approaching train. Shooting would stop, and all equipment would be cleared from the immediate area until the train passed. Once clear, everything was reset, and filming continued until the next designated train was due.

OPPOSITE BOTTOM LEFT The first day of shooting in Mobile, Alabama, at a Holiday Inn.

RIGHT On location, Spielberg and Truffaut discuss the Holiday Inn scene.

ABOVE At an Alabama railroad crossing, lights are put in place to simulate those from the UFO that hovers over Roy Neary's truck.

GLOVE COMPARTMENT POPS OPEN & VARIOUS INSTRUMENTS FLY OUT
PAPER CLIPS, PENS, ETC.

OBJECTS FLOAT FREELY.

ABOVE AND OPPOSITE BOTTOM LEFT Shooting Roy Neary's initial "close encounter."

LEFT A storyboard depicts the chaos inside Roy's truck as the UFO hovers overhead.

THESE PAGES Stills from a number of scenes that would be shot in Alabama but deleted from the final film. (Opposite top) Roy checks in with the power company crew to find miles of power lines have mysteriously disappeared; (opposite bottom) Roy starts to fill out a police report on his encounter at a local police station; (above) Roy stops to ask a crowd for directions during the power outage.

BELOW The crew films a piece of the scene in which Neary pursues the UFOs through a highway tunnel.

During the nocturnal shoot, for three nights in a row Spielberg filmed scenes that would ultimately be excised from the final version of *Close Encounters*. These included a scene in which, upon reaching one of the reported blackout areas, Neary is met by his colleagues from the power company, who show him the source of the problem. Neary looks up to see bare power poles against the starry skies—more than two miles of transmission and power wires have been removed, presumably by the alien visitors.

Also shot was a scene that finds Roy surrounded by a group of residents who are excited to see a representative from the power company. Monitoring radio chatter from both the police and the power company, he hears a report of an area that seemingly still has power, and speeds off to find it. Spielberg also shot a scene at the downtown Mobile police station that would follow a chase sequence in which Roy tails two police squad cars as they engage in a high-speed pursuit of three UFOs. In the scene that didn't make the final cut, Roy fills out a police report, but after seeing the two officers from the pursuit getting chewed out by their captain over their account of the incident, he gets discouraged and leaves.

The chase scene itself, in which Roy furiously pursues the police cars (with stunt coordinator Buddy Joe Hooker doubling for Dreyfuss on some of the more precarious high-speed maneuvers), would be filmed in a number of locations, and some shots were captured during the night shoot in Mobile. One particular shot filmed in Alabama saw Roy zip through a tunnel and a long stretch of highway. The set dressing department was called in to install a sign in the tunnel that indicated an exit for Harper Valley, a fictional location that sounded suitably Midwestern.

63

LEAVING RELIANCE

Moving from night to day, the production started the second week in Mobile with one of their biggest scenes to date—the complex and chaotic evacuation sequence set in the town of Reliance, Wyoming. "What makes a sequence difficult for the production team is how many moving pieces you have to deal with at any given time," says second AD Jim Bloom, who found that he lacked sufficient production staff to handle the difficult scene during the two-day shoot.

The small town of Bay Minette, some thirty-five miles from Mobile, would double for Reliance, the town being evacuated by the government under the pretense that there has been a toxic nerve gas spill in the area. In the script, Reliance was also the location where Roy and Jillian, having independently made a pilgrimage to Wyoming, run into each other and decide to travel together the rest of the journey to Devils Tower. The requirements for the scene, in addition to the main cast members, included one thousand extras plus cows, sheep, horses, hundreds of civilian cars, military vehicles, trucks, jeeps, personnel carriers, and the train and boxcars into which the populace would be loaded during the evacuation. When casting the background players, It was made clear to prospective extras that they would be required to work a twelve-hour day at the very least, and

if they weren't able to commit to two days at that location, they wouldn't be considered.

Although the main cast wouldn't be needed on set until 9 a.m., the day began at 6 a.m., when extras were scheduled to report to the hangar at Brookley Air Force Base to be processed by the hair, makeup, and wardrobe departments. From there, they would be shuttled over thirty miles to the set in Bay Minette. When everyone was assembled, along with the vehicles and animals to be used in the scene, first AD Chuck Myers and second AD Jim Bloom would meticulously choreograph the various beats of the sequence, in conjunction with Spielberg and cinematographer Vilmos Zsigmond. "There's a difference between a scene with one thousand extras standing still," explains Bloom, "and [one with] a thousand panicked extras loading on a train car with

TOP Actor Carl Weathers with Richard Dreyfuss during Weathers' one day of shooting on *Close Encounters*.

ABOVE (left to right) Spielberg, Phillips, and Dreyfuss during the Bay Minette shoot.

OPPOSITE TOP Spielberg directs his leading man during filming of the Reliance evacuation sequence.

OPPOSITE BOTTOM Melinda Dillon wades through the throng of extras during a Reliance evacuation scene.

64

military people, combined with the dynamic of what your leading man is doing." Along with the shots involving Dreyfuss, the scene was also shot from Neary's point of view as he first enters the area, taking in the mania and observing little vignettes occurring in various parts of the town, including an opportunistic vendor hawking gas masks and canaries.

In the midst of this chaotic sequence came a relatively calm interlude, courtesy of the scene when Roy is questioned by one of the soldiers protecting the area. The twenty-eight-year-old actor cast in the role, Carl Weathers, was a relative unknown in the film world, although he had made guest-starring roles in a number of popular television series. He would soon become a major star, playing Apollo Creed in the December 1976 release *Rocky*, which would go on to win the Oscar for Best Picture. Weathers recalls that he had finished shooting *Rocky* not long before getting the call about *Close Encounters*.

"I was home in Oakland, California, where I lived at the time," he says. "I got a call from my then-agent, saying there was this movie Steven Spielberg was doing, and they wanted me for a role, and it was a very small role, but as soon as I heard 'Steven Spielberg,' that kind of takes care of everything . . . I didn't have a script to read, and the only lines I was given were the lines that I was to say, so I didn't even get an entire scene. Still, it *was* Steven Spielberg."

Weathers jumped at the opportunity, despite the fact that he had precious little time to prepare for his role. "I literally got the lines

one day, hopped on a plane a day later, and went down to where they were shooting," he says. "I went to wardrobe and makeup, had a bite to eat, went to the set, and Steven and Rick Dreyfuss and I ran the lines a couple of times. Rick and I played tic-tac-toe on the top of a steel drum that was standing there as part of the set. Steven said 'action' and we shot it, and he did some coverage, and that was it. Went back to get cleaned up to go home. I got a chance to see the set in this large hangar that was built, got a short visit with Truffaut, and I was on a plane and back home within twenty-four hours. It was a whirlwind experience."

While Weathers' experience was short and sweet, what Melinda Dillon remembers most about those two days was the smell. "There was a paper factory there, and I don't know if you've ever smelled what it's like when you're making paper, but it's a very distinct, heavy smell," she says. "And there was no way you could get away from it. I remember wanting so much to get a breath of fresh air. And other than that, it was controlled chaos."

THESE PAGES Filming the evacuation of Reliance, Wyoming. In addition to the main action, Spielberg captured little snippets of the evacuees and even those taking advantage of the situation, including an opportunistic gas mask salesman.

HOME SWEET HOME

After the pandemonium of the evacuation scene, the company moved to the serenity of the suburbs—specifically, 1613 Carlisle Drive East, Mobile, where they officially welcomed Teri Garr and her onscreen kids to the production. Garr and the younger actors had already been in Mobile for over a week, being kept in reserve in case a change in the weather forced filming indoors. During that time, Garr had immersed herself in her role, interacting with women of Ronnie's age at various Mobile department stores and shopping centers. When choosing her wardrobe, she rejected anything that wasn't made from polyester, her research having led her to believe that the material was a clear favorite of housewives like Ronnie.

When they were first scouting Mobile to find a family home for the Nearys that could be used for both interior and exterior shots, Joe Alves and Clark Paylow had found the house on Carlisle Drive. At the time it was part of a housing community in the midst of development, where several of the newly built homes were not yet sold. Unfortunately, none of the properties were available for the production to lease. They came up with an alternative plan. Alves knew the amount of work that would have to be done on the house to make it ready for shooting,

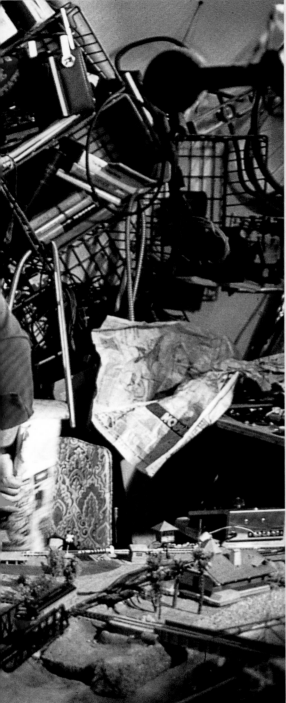

ABOVE Spielberg, Shawn Bishop, and Dreyfuss on the Neary home set.

TOP RIGHT In a scene that would be deleted from the final film, Ronnie Neary enjoys a moment with a friend at a neighborhood barbecue.

CENTER RIGHT Having reached her breaking point with Roy's erratic behavior, Ronnie Neary leaves with their kids.

including putting in a new lawn and decorating the interior. "Clark and I told the studio they could buy the house for $30,000, and we'd finish it up, and [after shooting, fix it up and] sell it for more," says Alves. "They said, 'Absolutely not!'"

However, when Alves announced that he and Paylow were going to personally buy the house themselves, lease it to the production for shooting, and resell it later at a considerable profit, Columbia had a quick change of heart and authorized the production to make the purchase.

Because of the gradual descent into disrepair that would occur in the home as a result of Roy's obsessive behavior, the scenes at the Nearys' house would be filmed in chronological order. The first footage to be shot would establish the family and their regular home life, with later scenes showing the house, and family, coming apart at the seams as Roy grows increasingly frenzied. Set decorator Phil Abramson found a model train store in Mobile where he purchased the railway models he would need for the elaborate dioramas being constructed in the Neary family room, designed to showcase Roy's hobbies as well as his obsession. Particular care went into the sculpting of the terrain surrounding the tracks, which would serve to establish Roy's craftsmanship and sculpting skills, talents that would come into play during his descent into UFO-related mania. Abramson packed the room with so many toys, tools, and other bits of paraphernalia that it was necessary to remove parts of the wall to give the camera enough room for the angles Spielberg needed. Teri Garr pitched in (with Spielberg's approval) and purchased assorted knickknacks to give the house a more personal touch.

The set dressing for these scenes was of utmost importance to Spielberg, who wanted to establish Roy's childlike nature and sense of wonder early in the film. This aspect of Roy's personality is also exemplified during the Neary house scene where he argues with his kids about going to see the animated classic *Pinocchio* rather than playing a round of Goofy Golf. The Disney film, and its connections to boyhood and the power of belief, would be referenced throughout *Close Encounters*.

Spielberg used the memory of being taken by his father to watch a meteor shower in the

middle of the night as the basis for the scene where Roy, after his first encounter, drags his wife and kids out of bed for a trip to Crescendo Summit. To further showcase Roy's spiral into apparent madness, Spielberg showed him beginning to sculpt the image he was seeing in his mind's eye using various everyday objects—mounds of shaving cream, pillows, and the infamous mashed potatoes. (In a deleted scene at a neighborhood block party, Roy became focused on a Jell-O mold.)

Each successive scene saw Spielberg take Roy from curiosity to frustration to anger and finally despair, culminating in an intensely emotional scene that found Dreyfuss huddled in the corner of the bathroom shower, water pouring down on him—a scene that would be cut from the original theatrical version of the film.

While shooting the breakdown scenes, Spielberg realized that Roy's frustrations needed to culminate in a eureka moment that would be clear to the audience, both thematically and visually. He found the perfect answer right in front of him in the form of a mountain that was part of Neary's model train diorama.

"He [Neary] had kept looking at it and

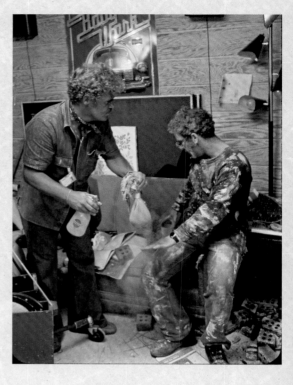

ABOVE A makeup artist applies dirt and grime to Dreyfuss for the scene where Neary sculpts a giant model of Devils Tower.

BELOW Spielberg and Dreyfuss walk through the scenes where an obsessed Neary tears up his yard to find sculpting materials.

OPPOSITE Neary's obsession manifests in shapes he begins to see in mounds of mashed potatoes, shaving cream, and (from a deleted scene) a Jell-O mold.

saying, 'This is not right,'" says Spielberg. "He was very frustrated, as something wasn't the way he imagined it needed to be." Spielberg had the art department make one modification to the model for the revised scene. "Out of frustration," he continues, "as he starts to tear his model apart, the top of the mountain comes off by accident. It flattens and looks exactly like the vision that he and the other people around the country have been implanted with."

For Dreyfuss, the scenes in the Neary home were both physically and emotionally draining, much more so than in his previous collaboration with Spielberg. "*Jaws* wasn't difficult in terms of the physical; it was tough in terms of patience," says Dreyfuss. "It was all about the waiting: waiting for the shot to clear, waiting for the shark to work, waiting for the shark not to work. But *Close Encounters . . .* running through the garden and throwing shit in the windows, and then building [the mountain], letting yourself be possessed by this image and then humiliating yourself in front of your children . . . It was a very emotional experience, but it was just something you wallowed in. You just surrendered. And behind my head all the time was that word—*noble*. This is worth it!"

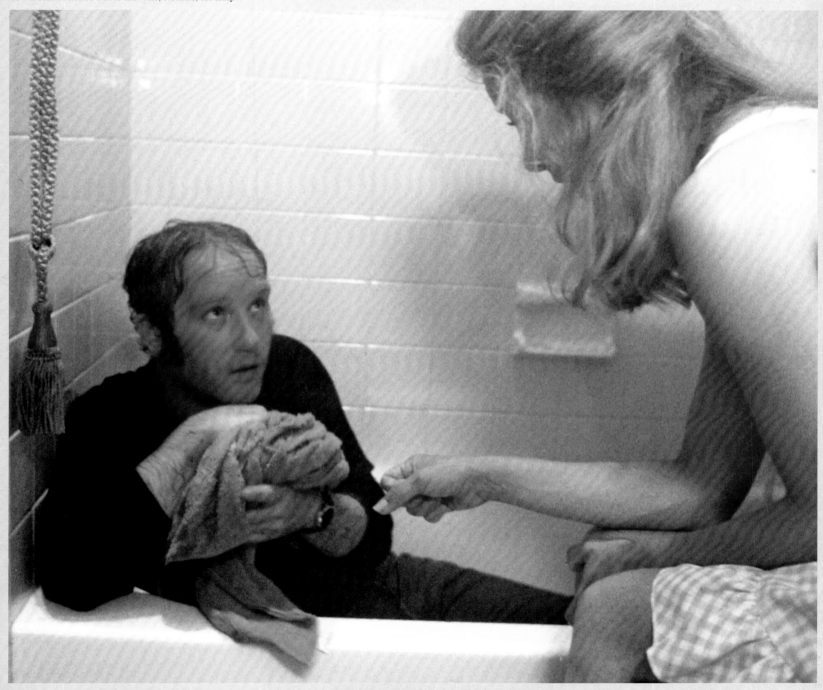

LANGUAGE BARRIERS

Since opening in 1964, the Municipal Auditorium in Mobile had been home to live performances by Elvis Presley, the Jackson 5, Chicago, the Rolling Stones, the Monkees, Stevie Wonder, Bruce Springsteen, and Elton John, among many others. On June 28, 1976, it housed the *Close Encounters* crew, who were there to film a scene where Lacombe addresses a group of scientists and military personnel on the latest Mayflower Project breakthrough.

Spielberg insisted that Truffaut perform the entire scene in English, which, given the large amount of dialogue in the scene, worried the Frenchman. Balaban helped Truffaut rehearse and helpfully corrected his pronunciation when needed. When the time came to shoot, he performed the first takes admirably, but when Spielberg went in for a close-up, Truffaut began to stumble over the word "today." Spielberg kept the cameras rolling until Truffaut halted mid-sentence, looked up with a smile, and proclaimed, "Ziss is terrible!" to the amusement of the director and the crew. Despite the momentary snafu, Truffaut ultimately gave Spielberg the exact performance he needed.

Just weeks before this scene was shot, it had been revised to include a moment where Lacombe demonstrates Kodály hand signals for the assembled group in conjunction with a recording of villagers in India chanting the Five Notes. "John Williams came up with that," says Spielberg. "He had heard of the Kodály hand signs to teach music to people that were hearing-impaired or deaf . . . And John was the one that brought that to my attention."

"I may have seen some demonstrations of hand positions that indicated sound or color," the composer recalls. "[I told Spielberg about] Zoltán Kodály, [who designed] the hand signals

for the deaf. We could never be sure that these extraterrestrials actually could hear anything."

One of the assembled Mayflower Project team members, referred to on the call sheet as Team Leader, was portrayed by an alumnus of Spielberg's *Sugarland Express.* Merrill Connally, a native of Floresville, Texas, was the brother of John Connally, former governor of Texas. Spielberg had enjoyed having Connally on *Sugarland,* and although he was only supposed to be part of that one scene in *Close Encounters,* the director decided to add him to the entire Box Canyon/arrival scene, giving him snippets of dialogue originally earmarked for other characters.

While the crew shot the conference scene in Mobile, Joe Alves used the time to carry out some much-needed work on Roy's painfully detailed, living room–size sculpture of Devils Tower. Created by plaster and fiberglass expert George Sampson (on loan to Alves from Paramount Pictures) the model stood over nine feet tall and was made from Styrofoam and chicken wire and covered in plaster. Sampson and the art department crew built the model in the hangar at Brookley Air Force Base and transported it to the set. Their one minor miscalculation in the process was that the model was too big to fit through the doors (or windows) of the house.

TOP Lacombe demonstrates the Kodály hand signals during a Mayflower Project conference.

ABOVE Spielberg directs Truffaut during the conference scene.

OPPOSITE A makeshift set was built in the Mobile hangar for the scene where Roy is interrogated by Lacombe and Laughlin.

Alves had to slice the model in half in order to move it indoors, and then glued it back together in time for filming.

The final scene captured at the Neary house would be the moment where Roy recognizes Devils Tower as the subject of his visions when he glimpses the landmark in a news report about the evacuation taking place in the area. The news report itself was filmed during the Wyoming shoot.

After leaving the Neary home, the company moved to the Mobile Aerospace Complex to shoot two scenes: the first meeting of Lacombe and Laughlin, and an Air Force official's investigation into a commercial jet's midair encounter with a UFO. The scene with Truffaut and Balaban, set in the confines of a limousine, would attempt to bring some levity to the proceedings as Lacombe asks Laughlin to translate a

semi-pornographic passage from a French book to determine his proficiency in the language.

In his very first draft of the script, Spielberg had written a scene in which the American version of Lacombe boarded a commercial jet that had encountered a UFO to confiscate any recording devices belonging to the passengers aboard the flight. The scene remained in the final draft, but Spielberg transposed the action to the character of the Air Force official.

In the end, neither of the scenes would end up onscreen. Spielberg deemed the interrogation of the passengers unnecessary to the action, and Claude Lacombe and David Laughlin would meet again under different circumstances after a future script revision.

Because of the limited number of shooting days at Devils Tower, Spielberg

was forced to move a key sequence that was supposed to be shot at the Wyoming location to the Mobile portion of the shoot. That scene, in which Lacombe and Laughlin interview Roy Neary at the Army encampment, required the art department to recreate the interior of a trailer in a hangar adjacent to the "Big Set" at Brookley Air Force Base.

Because he considered this to be a critical scene, Spielberg had rewritten it many times, finishing the final version just before leaving for the set. He rode over with Truffaut and Balaban and went over the dialogue with them on their way to the hangar. For Truffaut, who had only one line in English, the changes weren't of much concern, but Balaban needed time to translate the lines into French, and wouldn't have enough time to learn all of them before shooting. As Truffaut had done back in Wyoming with manila envelopes, Balaban asked an AD to bring him a large piece of

cardboard on which he jotted down the lines, and quickly nailed the scene as a result.

But the threat of flubbed lines turned out to be the least of the production's problems that day. When Richard Dreyfuss arrived to film the scene, he was accompanied by several armed bodyguards. As the American bicentennial celebration neared, Dreyfuss had been infuriated to hear that the local Ku Klux Klan chapter was planning to march through Mobile on the Fourth of July. Eager to show his disdain, Dreyfuss sought the advice of Al Ebner, the film's publicist. "He said, 'The most effective thing for you to do is make a statement to the [Associated Press] wire, and they'll read it off on TV.' And sure enough, that's what happened."

Dreyfuss's statement left no room for doubt on where the actor stood: "Under the Constitution of the United States, the Ku Klux Klan has every right to march through the city of Mobile on July 4th, and under that same Constitution and Bill of Rights, I have the right to call them a bunch of thugs." Dreyfuss's release was read by newscasters on two stations.

"Within ten minutes, [I got] two death threats," the actor says, recalling the immediate reaction to his statement. "I called Julia Phillips, and she had a security agency wrapped around my house [in Alabama] in ten minutes. They didn't know why they were hired, but they were everywhere. They were in cars, in trees, and there was a guy in my house, and he had a dog and a shotgun. He was sitting in my kitchen, and we're talking general politics. He does not know why he had been hired. He just knows he's there to protect my life. And in the course of the conversation, he says, 'Oh, I've been in the Klan now for eight or nine years.'" Dreyfuss politely excused himself and put in another call to Julia Phillips, who had him taken immediately to the set.

Although fully supportive of the stance his friend had taken, Bob Balaban was a little concerned about his own resemblance to Dreyfuss. "I went to Julia Phillips and I said, 'You know, Julia, a lot of people in this area kind of think that I'm Richard Dreyfuss and maybe you could get me, maybe not a bunch of guards, but maybe I could have one guard, you know, in case somebody decides to kill me?'" says Balaban. "And she said, 'Bob, I really like you, but if Richard gets shot, the whole movie is over. If you get shot, we can deal with it.' She was sort of joking, but of course it was the absolute truth."

After they wrapped the scene, Dreyfuss and Balaban both hopped on planes to New York for the holiday weekend. Balaban in particular was glad to be home for a few days. "I got to see a lot of the bicentennial activities in New York, which was lovely," he says. "And I also didn't get killed."

MEET THE GUILERS

A farmhouse in Fairhope, just outside Mobile, had been chosen as the location for the Guiler house, where young Barry would be abducted by the aliens.

Before shooting could start, Spielberg first had to decide which toddler would play the role of Barry. He had flown both Zack Bowman and Cary Guffey to the location so that he could direct each of them in a test scene: the moment when Barry walks down the stairs to find that the alien visitors have left the house in disarray. Melinda Dillon was on hand to observe the audition process. "Steven was telling them to do stuff and see how well they responded," she recalls. "Zack had already decided it was his world, and he was going to take it. He was this rough-and-tumble kid, and he wouldn't do anything Steven said, or mind his mother. I really liked Zack. And Cary was this wondrous, quiet, soft, attentive, listening child from Georgia. And I know that's one of the things you learn when you're a baby in the South. You learn how to be a very sweet, good little person."

Although Spielberg liked Zack's energy, he was quickly won over by young Cary, who had just turned four a few weeks earlier. "Cary had a look in his eye that Norman Rockwell would have captured to represent a child getting his first

tricycle at Christmas," says Spielberg. "He had the Rockwell eye sparkle, a crooked little smile, and I completely went for him in this role."

With the decision made, Cary was on set to begin shooting the very next day. As with the filming at the Neary house, all the scenes captured at the Guiler residence would be shot sequentially, starting with Barry waking up to find his toys have come to life. In order to get the most realistic performance from Cary, the youngster was put down for a nap in the character's bed on set, while the crew patiently waited for him to fall asleep so they could set up the shot. "I didn't think he could fake being tired and pretending at four years old to be startled by something and still look tired," says Spielberg. "[So] we let him go to sleep, and he was sleeping soundly. We quietly lit him with three lights, set up the camera and gently woke him. What's on film is a four-year-old boy waking up."

"One of the guys bumped into the bed and I woke up," says Guffey, who opened his eyes to find himself surrounded by a large group of people. "Lighting, sound, assistant director,

TOP LEFT A dilapidated farmhouse outside Mobile was refurbished by Alves and his team to serve as the home of Jillian and Barry Guiler.

ABOVE Jillian and Barry huddle together as the ETs make their presence felt.

OPPOSITE BOTTOM LEFT Storyboards depict Jillian looking up in alarm as she sees the approaching spacecraft.

OPPOSITE TOP RIGHT As Cary Guffey naps in his onscreen bed, a camera is silently moved into position to authentically capture the moment he awakes.

JILLIAN LEAVES HOUSE, COMES FORWARD TO CARRY OUT GARBAGE.

JILL'S P.O.V. BARRY ON PORCH

JILLIAN LOOKS UP AT THE SKY.

wardrobe, camera, director. All these people in this itty-bitty room. Waking up to that was just a real response. I can't really say it was acting as much as it was responding to, 'Okay, this is weird. Where did all these people come from?'"

To bring Barry's toys to life, Roy Arbogast turned to one of his crew members, who modified store-bought toys to "wake up" for the scene. "He was very good at electronics, and he put timers in all of them," says Arbogast. "We'd run in, and set them all off, and everything would run at the same time."

What Guffey remembers most about his time on set is his relationship with Spielberg, who treated him with warmth and respect. "He was like a big kid, almost like a big brother," says Guffey, who left show business early in his life and grew up to become a financial consultant. "It was 'Hey, let's hang out, let's have a good time.' It was him giving me gifts and taking me for a ride on his motorcycle. He never treated me like a kid, per se. He interacted with me continually, and he explained things."

"I did that because he heard me with different ears," Spielberg says. "There are some kids you really can't sit down and speak to the way I would speak to Richard Dreyfuss or Melinda Dillon. Cary was somebody you could have a conversation with, and he was wise beyond his years. He was a lot of fun, and he loved to role-play. He loved nothing more than to allow me to play tricks on him. At four years old, I would never call Cary an actor. He

was still very much himself, and I needed what he was showing me behind the scenes, in front of the lens. And often, to do that, the same kind of games we would play when we weren't shooting were the games I began playing with Cary in front of the camera."

One of those games would come into play when shooting the scene that immediately followed the shot of Barry waking up. Going down to the kitchen, the boy is surprised to find the contents of the refrigerator spilled all over the floor. Spielberg needed to get a number of different emotions from Cary in this moment. He dressed one of the crew members as a clown, and makeup supervisor Bob Westmoreland as a gorilla, and put them on opposite ends of the room, hidden by large pieces of cardboard. When Cary entered the room and hit his mark, he surveyed the mess, and then looked up. The first crew member dropped his piece of cardboard to reveal his clown costume. Startled, Cary started to smile. A few seconds later, Spielberg gave Westmoreland the signal to drop his cardboard, revealing the gorilla suit, and Cary reflexively took a step back, alarmed. Spielberg whispered for Westmoreland to take off the head, and when Cary recognized the makeup supervisor under the mask, he broke into a wide grin, a moment that in the final film would be used as Barry's reaction to seeing the aliens offscreen. Both this and the waking-up scene were achieved to Spielberg's satisfaction on the first

79

take, a fortunate outcome since the surprise element would only have worked once.

When shooting at the Guiler house, Spielberg's directorial surprises weren't confined to Cary Guffey. Roy Arbogast remembers getting a call from the director with very explicit instructions for prepping the scene where Barry is actually taken by the aliens: "He said, 'I want you to go out to that house, and do whatever you can in that kitchen, and nobody is to know what to expect.'" Arbogast and his crew went to work, rigging the kitchen with various effects, many of them powered by pneumatics, like those that animated the mailboxes and stop sign for the railroad crossing scene. "We had a lot of cylinders rigged under the appliances," he explains. As he turned up the power, the appliances would shake even more violently, the refrigerator door vibrating open and the contents spilling to the floor. Amongst other effects, knives would fly out of the dishwasher (at a safe distance from the actors), and smoke wafted up though the vents as the house lights flickered on and off. An eerie scene showing screws spontaneously

working their way out of a floor vent would be captured in postproduction back in Burbank. "That was my ten-year-old son at the time," says Arbogast, "[lying] under the set with a screwdriver, backing them out."

Just before he was ready to begin shooting the kitchen sequence, Spielberg took Cary aside and explained what was going to happen. "I remember him . . . showing me the controls for how the kitchen would blow apart," says Guffey. "And he did it intentionally because he didn't want me to be scared when everything went crazy."

Spielberg also told Cary that the set mechanics were a secret that should be kept

OPPOSITE Spielberg shows Cary Guffey around the Guiler home set.

ABOVE Mechanical effects supervisor Roy Arbogast rigged the kitchen appliances to violently shake and rattle during the abduction scene.

TOP RIGHT Spielberg examines one of the specially rigged toys that will come to life when the aliens arrive.

BELOW Cary Guffey in the scene where Barry finds the kitchen in disarray.

from Dillon, his screen mom. "That's the genius of Spielberg," he continues. "Rather than saying, 'Oh he's a four-year-old kid, he's not going to understand anything. Why bother?,' he actually took the time to show me how it was going to work, and explained to me, 'We have control of it.' That's why I had no fear in those scenes where the kitchen is coming apart. To me, it was like a big joke on Melinda Dillon."

When the actress got to the set, Spielberg informed her they were not going to rehearse the sequence and would instead go straight to filming. When he called "action" and the pneumatic devices started firing, Spielberg got exactly the reactions of abject terror from Dillon that he had hoped for. "I made sure I had two cameras on her, so I wouldn't miss it," Spielberg says. "And she didn't disappoint me!"

Reflecting on the scene decades later, Dillon doesn't question Spielberg's tactics. "It worked," she says. "It was terrifying. It was just frightening to have this thing fall apart around you, and it was very noisy and loud."

Fortunately, despite the chaos, the actress did have enough presence of mind to follow the one piece of direction that Spielberg had stressed before the scene began. "I was told, you've got to let him [Cary] go," she recalls. "He's got to go through that [doggy] door, and he's got to go through that door by this time. So my job was to justify somehow opening my arms up, and him being able to get out [of my embrace]. So that was very tricky, within my own head, to be able to get so distracted by the house falling down, to let my son out of my arms for a second."

As the scene continued, Cary did indeed get to crawl through the doggy door, while Dillon tried to pull him back in. "Again, trying to keep me from being afraid, my real mom was on the other side of the door, doing the tug-of-war with Melinda," says Guffey. "To me, there was nothing to it. I just crawled through a doggy door, and there's my real mom waiting to pull me through. It was a game, and not in the least bit scary. To simplify it, the set was like playtime for me."

THE BIG SET

It took Joe Alves and his crew three months to complete construction on the Box Canyon set at the Brookley Air Force Base dirigible hangar. The first step had been to extend the area in which they could film by opening up one set of hangar doors, which added an additional 150 feet of space to the original 300 feet. They then draped the custom-made tarp around the complex. The tarp itself was made of nylon and was black on the side that would be visible on set and white on the reverse. The black side would give the illusion that the climax of the film was taking place outside under the night sky, while the white side would deflect the intense Alabama summer heat. To hold the tarps in place, an elaborate steel scaffolding structure was erected outside the hangar.

Despite the fact that the dirigible hangar was designed to easily hold the weight of large aircraft, Alves put down another layer of concrete on the floor of the hangar to ensure that the additional tonnage of the filming equipment, set materials, and crew wouldn't test its limits. In addition, the new concrete had been embedded with fluorescent lights as part of the high-tech set design. Practical electrical outlets were also installed around the set to power the scientific equipment that would be visible in the final scenes. During his research for the Box Canyon scene, Alves quizzed a number of scientists on the type of equipment that might be used if a project of this nature existed. In addition to incorporating their suggestions into his designs for the prop equipment, he rented four control consoles from NASA's Johnson Space Center in Houston, which would be used prominently on the set. Production sound mixer Gene Cantamessa would record the sounds made by these consoles, which would later be used by supervising sound effects editor Frank E. Warner in postproduction.

Because the Box Canyon landing site was supposed to be outdoors and situated at Devils Tower, three sides of the set needed to be filled with fake rocks to maintain the illusion. Alves had George Sampson make the molds in Los Angeles, and then in Mobile had six thousand prop rocks fabricated from 14,000 square feet of fiberglass.

Another prominent feature of the set was the large, scoreboard-style light board that would flash in unison with the musical notes generated by the assembled scientists attempting to communicate with the Mothership. Alves's concept for the device was rooted in musical theory. He based the board on the twelve-tone musical technique, a musical scale with twelve pitches, and then assigned a six-color palette to each note, ending up with a total of seventy-two panels, each having its own colored light. "We wired them to a keyboard so we could actually play the colors of the various tones," says Alves. After they were played for Spielberg and John Williams, the director made a few aesthetic changes to the placement of the various colors that would flash across the surface of the board.

Although Vilmos Zsigmond's research trip to the Rose Bowl had given him hope that he would be able to illuminate the set using just the lights that were part of the production

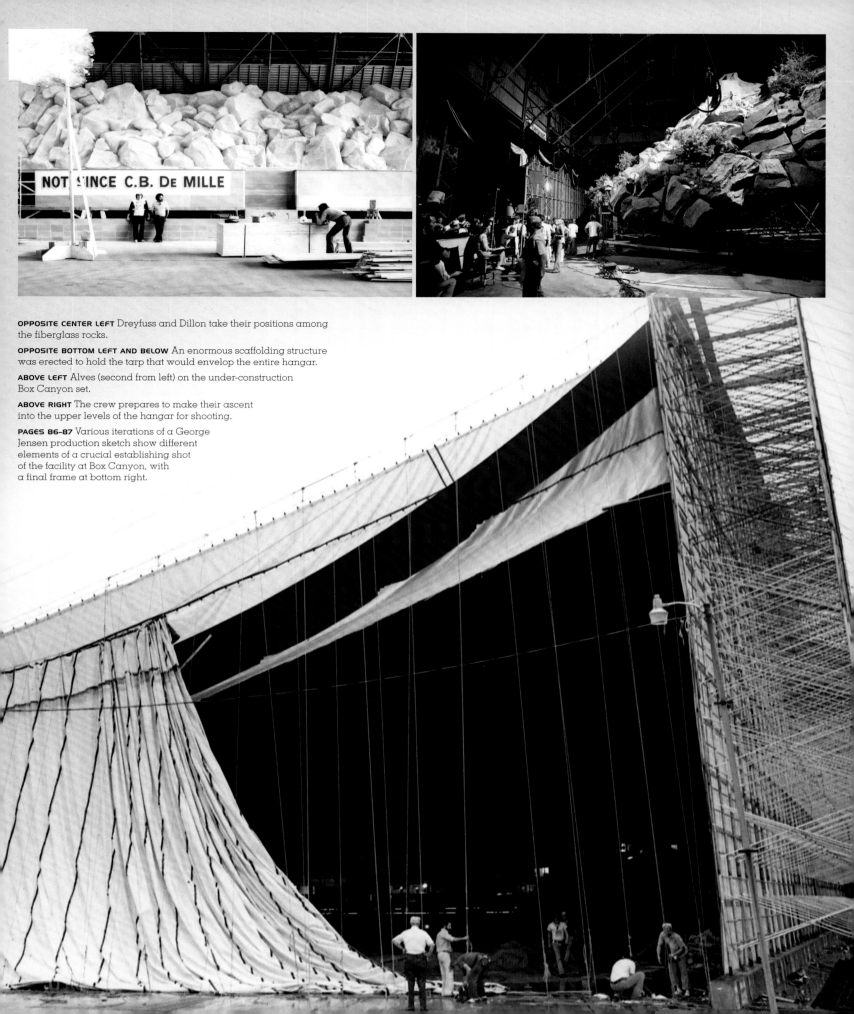

OPPOSITE CENTER LEFT Dreyfuss and Dillon take their positions among the fiberglass rocks.

OPPOSITE BOTTOM LEFT AND BELOW An enormous scaffolding structure was erected to hold the tarp that would envelop the entire hangar.

ABOVE LEFT Alves (second from left) on the under-construction Box Canyon set.

ABOVE RIGHT The crew prepares to make their ascent into the upper levels of the hangar for shooting.

PAGES 86–87 Various iterations of a George Jensen production sketch show different elements of a crucial establishing shot of the facility at Box Canyon, with a final frame at bottom right.

NOT SINCE C.B. De MILLE

OPPOSITE TOP LEFT AND OPPOSITE TOP RIGHT
Sections of Devils Tower begin to take shape
on the Box Canyon set.

OPPOSITE BOTTOM Richard Dreyfuss takes a
break near a completed section of the mountain.

BOTTOM LEFT A view from the back of the Box
Canyon set looking out toward the immense
hangar doors that would be covered with a
tarp for shooting.

CENTER RIGHT Spielberg began shooting the
scenes of Box Canyon from the very top of the
makeshift soundstage.

BOTTOM RIGHT Perched on the fiberglass rocks,
Spielberg and Dillon discuss a scene.

PAGES 90–91 The final shot of Roy and Jillian
looking down on Box Canyon was made up
of a number of different elements which were
later combined in postproduction.

design, when he first stepped onto the Box
Canyon set he realized that this plan was
inadequate. The same lights that illuminated
a full football stadium would look flat within
the great expanse of the hangar. Therefore, to
augment the light stanchions Alves was using
as part of the set design, Zsigmond would
need to situate a panoply of lights of varying
brilliance behind the scenes and in the rafters.

Not only did Zsigmond have to solve the
problem of lighting the set, but he also had
to figure out how the dynamic lighting that
emanated from the UFOs would bathe the
area and the Box Canyon technicians. Cranes
would swing some lights across the set, and
the construction team devised an overhead
monorail system, hung from the superstructure
of the hangar, on which a series of lights could
travel. Up in the rafters, forty-eight separate
high-intensity arc lights were suspended, each
manned by a member of the crew. Columbia's
Stanley Jaffe recalls inspecting the setup: "It was
impressive what they were doing, but it was
also concerning because the DP . . . had shipped
two [very expensive] Coast Guard lights from
San Diego, which they were going to put up on
walkways about forty feet above the floor, and
were going to pan them. They weighed about a

couple of tons each. Panning them wasn't going
to be an option, so they weren't used."

At the end of the production, Alves
estimated that the Box Canyon set was built at
a cost of $700,000. The raw materials included
more than ten miles of lumber, three and a
half miles of steel scaffolding, two miles of
fiberglass, and the mile-long tarp, as well as
tons of concrete, sand, and clay fill dirt. Vilmos
Zsigmond proclaimed it not only the biggest
set on which he'd ever worked, but in all prob-
ability the biggest set ever created at the time.
"The set was so big that you couldn't stand in

the middle and shout out to the edges," adds
camera operator/second unit DP Steven Poster.

The enormous set was also subject to
stringent security to protect the film's secrets,
with guards posted both inside and outside
the hangar. All cast and crew were required to
wear photo ID badges provided by production,
and no one was exempt from this rule. On
various occasions, Dreyfuss, Balaban, and
even Spielberg were stopped because they had
misplaced their badges. It was only after calls
to the production office for clearance that they
were allowed onto the set.

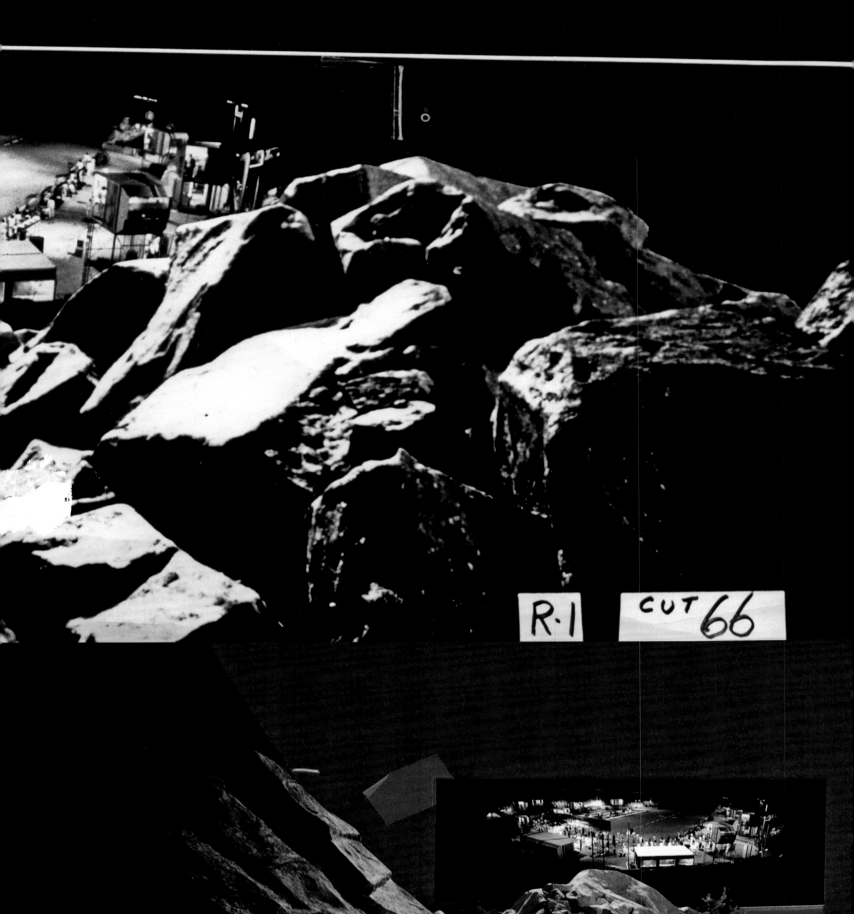

SHOOTING THE "GRAND" CANYON

Shooting on the Box Canyon set would be divided into two sections—the first being the preparation for the arrival of the ETs, and the second, the touchdown of the Mothership and the historic first meeting between mankind and the aliens.

Given that the Box Canyon shoot would be so complex, Spielberg wanted to break down each moment of the sequence for the crew. He had already gone over every planned shot with production illustrator George Jensen, who in turn sketched well over a hundred storyboards of the action. Every storyboard was numbered and lettered, with each panel showing the action to be filmed,

along with notations on camera angles and any special effects equipment necessary for that shot. The storyboards were tacked up along a wall of the hangar in the order in which they were to be shot, and the call sheet listed the number of storyboards that would be shot each day. "I made up a lot of shots in between the assigned storyboards," Spielberg admits. "But we basically used the

storyboards to guide us through that difficult portion of production."

Spielberg decided the best way to begin the shoot was to take it from the top of the nine-story hangar for the scene where Roy and Jillian, having scaled Devils Tower, emerge at the top of Box Canyon. The first few shots began with Spielberg and his camera crew filming an overview of the set from almost one hundred feet in the air, giving the audience the first reveal of the massive complex from Roy and Jillian's point of view. As the scene progressed, Spielberg would follow Roy and Jillian as they slowly made their way down the rocks of the canyon wall to join the action at the facility below.

With the descent scenes complete, Spielberg would return to the stage floor to film the Mayflower Project team's reaction to the appearance of three alien scout ships, heralding the imminent arrival of the Mothership. Spielberg and Zsigmond used powerful studio lights to create the illumination emanating from each UFO. Each light was tagged with a number so that when Spielberg called out a specific digit, the cast and the extras would react to that light in unison. A combination of wind machines and small personal blowers provided the

EFFECT #70 LACOMBE RIM LIT ANGLE TOWARD BASE OF MOUNTAIN

LIVE ACTION SET

FRONT-PROJECTION PLATE SKY EFFECTS + MATTE MOUNT

TOP Spielberg takes a break from filming on the massive Box Canyon set.

ABOVE George Jensen's storyboards depict Lacombe observing the approach of the UFOs.

LEFT François Truffaut on the Box Canyon set.

OPPOSITE TOP Various angles of the scientific installation, including elevated views from the fiberglass rocks.

OPPOSITE BOTTOM Scientist extras react to the arrival of the UFOs. In the background, the cubicles built by Alves's construction crew can be seen.

physical on-set effect of the ships flying close above the onlookers.

Since Spielberg intended to film this key moment from many different angles and elevations, the action would need to be repeated dozens of times and would have to match from take to take. This would require the many extras to perform their actions without variation again and again, not only for the sake of continuity and editing, but also to help with the blending of visual effects and live-action footage in postproduction.

To make this repetitive task a little easier, first assistant director Chuck Myers went to all of the cubicles the technician extras were posted at, gave each of the extras a character name, and invented specific stories for them. He also showed them how to operate various pieces of the prop scientific equipment and patiently explained the movements they would need to repeat, take after take.

Before shooting the Box Canyon scenes, the cast and crew were alerted that conditions in the hangar were going to be very uncomfortable. The Mobile summer was at full July strength, with on-set temperatures starting at over 100 degrees and rising even higher due to the myriad lights bearing down from the rafters. Air conditioning would be provided whenever possible, but the sheer enormity of the set prevented the units from providing comprehensive cooling for the entire area. Additionally, the air conditioning had to be regulated as it would dissipate the output of the smoke machines which filled the set with an appropriately atmospheric haze each morning.

More than 150 extras were used in the sequence, among them Dreyfuss's father,

Norman, who would man one of the technician cubicles alongside Balaban and Truffaut. When he told his son that he wanted to appear in the film, the younger Dreyfuss tried to discourage him, explaining that the job entailed extremely long hours in an uncomfortable, overheated environment, with precious little excitement to be had. But Norman would not be deterred.

Also appearing as an extra was Phil Dodds, who came to the production as a representative of ARP Instruments, the company whose ARP 2500 keyboard-based music synthesizer appears in the film. Spielberg met Dodds when he was installing and testing the equipment and asked him if he wanted to appear in the film as the ARP operator who plays the hallowed five-note tune when the Mothership arrives. During shooting, Spielberg would upgrade Dodds to a speaking role (although his dialogue was later cut) and name his character Jean Claude.

TOP ARP Instruments representative Phil Dodds (left) stands by as Spielberg takes a turn on the synthesizer. Dodds would play the synthesizer onscreen in the film.

LEFT On the Box Canyon set, Spielberg directs Lance Henriksen, Truffaut, and Balaban.

OPPOSITE TOP Lacombe rushes to take his position as the UFOs make their first appearance.

OPPOSITE BOTTOM Extras feel the effects of the portable air blowers used to simulate the downdraft generated by the arriving UFOs.

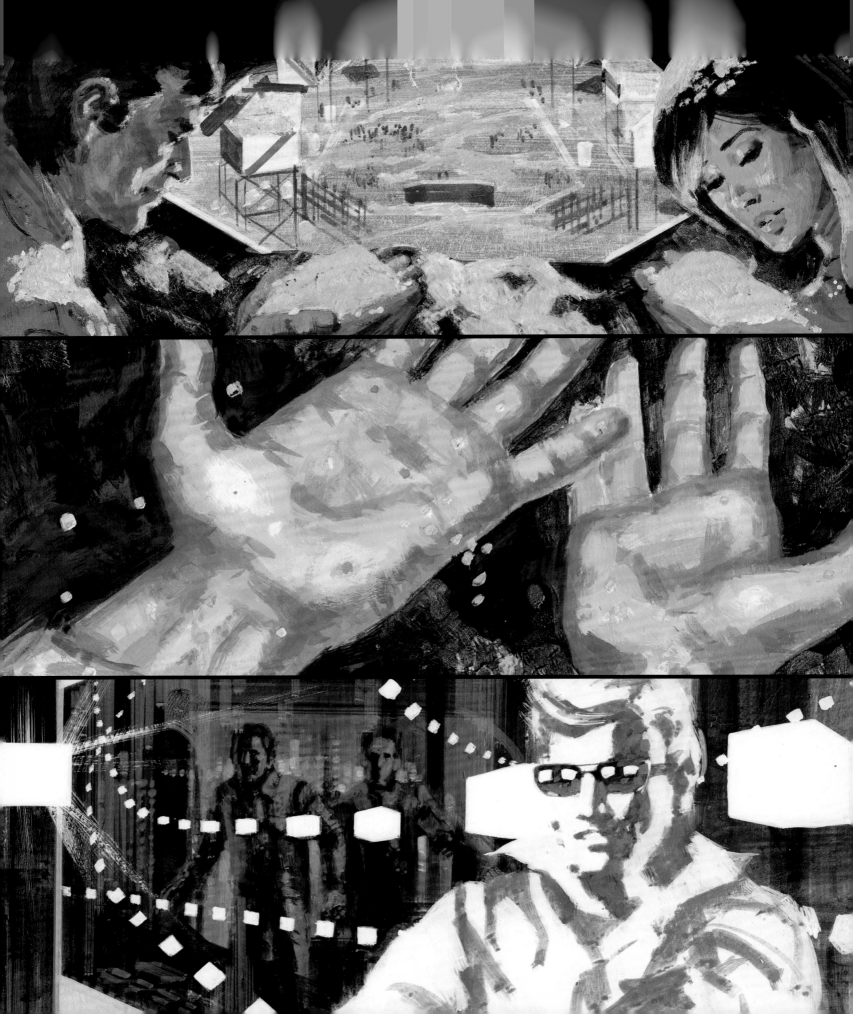

TECHNICAL DIFFICULTIES / NATURE CALLS

In the final draft of his shooting script, Spielberg detailed an elaborate five-page scene that, while enchanting on paper, would prove to be too technically challenging to realize. The sequence introduced the "cuboids," dozens and dozens of illuminated cubes that were dispersed by the three scout ships at the landing strip. These objects would fly all around the complex, interacting with the technicians and "posing" for the cameras that were recording the event. When a camera flashed a red light, signifying that it was out of film, the cuboids would move on. When they reached their zenith, they would burst into "galactic golden dust that races in all directions" and envelop the assembled spectators. In the script, the last remaining cuboid interacted directly with Neary during a particularly spectacular moment:

THESE PAGES Paintings by production illustrator George Jensen bring to life the deleted "cuboids" sequence, as the tiny cubes depart the ships and interact with the humans.

The micro cube does something extraordinary. It finds its way underneath the skin in Roy's open palm without the slightest twinge of pain. He watches as it travels around the inside of his hand, up a finger, down to the wrist, into a vein. The vein glows bright blue as the speck of light runs its course around the hand and finally, sadly, fades out, leaving everything dark and silent and mystical.

Spielberg had detailed elaborate moves for the cuboid action, with the entities flying in various formations throughout the canyon. "It was almost like a *Fantasia* [dance sequence] kind of thing," recalls Douglas Trumbull. "That was one of the areas that we had thought would be most suitable for computer graphics." However, given that computer technology for filmmaking was still in its infancy at the time, Spielberg and the team decided to try to create the scene using practical effects.

Roy Arbogast and his crew built a number of the cuboids from plastic boxes fitted with high-intensity light bulbs. They then strung the set with a series of electrified wires on which the boxes would travel. Kevin Pike, who had first worked part-time for Arbogast on *Jaws*,

and then became a full-time member of the *Close Encounters* effects crew, recalls working on the cuboids. "We made a lot of them travel in straight lines, just like subway cars going by you at high speed and making a flicker effect," says Pike, "but we could never make them go in a curved direction." The special effects team also found that the intensity of the set lights caused the wires to heat up and sag, derailing the boxes. "We constantly had issues with trying to get that worked out and make the cuboids travel," continues Pike. "We got them going at a pretty high speed. There was a lot of electricity out there. [We] had to make sure that the cast and the extras didn't walk into that wire when the cuboids were traveling by."

Bob Balaban was one of the cast members tasked with gazing wondrously at the special effects team's cuboid creations. "We were given strict instructions not to touch the cuboids, because each of them had like twelve million volts of electricity, and we would have been electrocuted," he recalls. "And we're sort of sitting there thinking, 'Well, we're not going

97

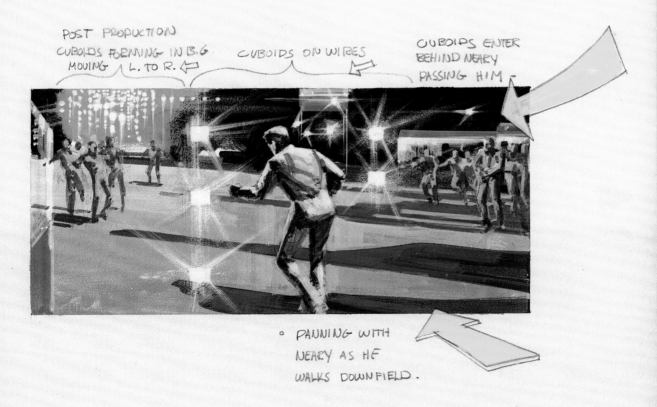

POST PRODUCTION
CUBOIDS FORMING IN B.G.
MOVING L. TO R. ⇐

CUBOIDS ON WIRES

CUBOIDS ENTER
BEHIND NEARY
PASSING HIM —

○ PANNING WITH
NEARY AS HE
WALKS DOWNFIELD.

① OPERAT
③
3RD CUBOI
⑤

to touch them, but what if they fall on us or somebody makes a mistake?' We did that for a couple of days."

"We didn't know how to do it," admits Spielberg. "We tried it. We put them on wires. The problem was, the cuboids were like little Chinese lanterns. Very small, but they lit the wires that they were traveling down, and this was the analog era of film, before digital wire removal was invented. It was an effect that I thought would work, but wound up, on a day of practical production, not working at all."

Unfortunately, the decision to abandon the scene also led to the deletion of Douglas Trumbull's cameo as one of the technicians who interacts with the cuboids.

During those first weeks in the Box Canyon set, the crew also fell afoul of the elements. Summer storms were not uncommon in Mobile, but since the shooting was being carried out indoors, it was not thought to be a problem. One day, while filming his reaction to the scout ships, Bob Balaban looked to the far end of the hangar and saw a tiny piece of daylight leaking through the black tarp. The pinpoint of light began to grow slowly, until the tarp ripped open, exposing the set to the gale force winds that had split the material. A tremendous storm had enveloped the area. While the crew scrambled to salvage the enormous tarp, François Truffaut's directorial instincts kicked in, and he lifted his hands to his eyes in order to frame the tumultuous scene. He was later disappointed to find out that Spielberg's cameras had not captured the fury of the storm.

In the aftermath of this setback, the schedule was rearranged to allow Alves's crew to repair the tarp so that shooting could continue. While that was being done, Spielberg took the production back to the Neary house for some additional shots of Roy tearing up the yard for materials with which to build his mountain. After returning to the hangar and completing the scene interrupted by the storm, they once again moved out to allow rigging to be put into place for the construction of the Mothership set.

THESE PAGES Additional Jensen production art and storyboards for the cuboids sequence.

2

...TING THINGS IN BRIEFCASE —

1ST CUBOID ENTERS, 2ND ENTERS, HE DOESN'T BUDGE

4

...RS — HE CONTINUES PACKING.

THEY TURN RED & BUZZ, HE NODS GOODBYE, CLOSES BRIEFCASE.

HE EXITS THE SHOT AS THE CUBOIDS FLASH THROUGH THE SPECTRUM IN CELEBRATION.   SAVE

A CHANGE OF VENUE

After moving to the adjacent, smaller hangar, the first piece of action to be filmed was a scene that Spielberg had added at the last minute. Having already shot Roy watching the newscast that revealed Devils Tower, Spielberg felt that Jillian should have her own moment of recognition, seeing that same telecast from another location. He envisioned her in a motel room somewhere in New Mexico, during her search for her kidnapped son.

Joe Alves called upon experience gained from his television days on such series as *Night Gallery* to construct a basic three-walled motel room set, decorated in the Southwestern motif, the walls adorned with dozens of Jillian's sketches of Devils Tower (drawn by production illustrator George Jensen.) Spielberg was more than satisfied with the set, but Alves also received unexpected high praise from François Truffaut. While the French director never once seemed impressed by Alves's massive Box Canyon set, he was curiously enthusiastic about this much less complex construction. "He walked on this little three-walled structure," says Alves, "and he goes, 'Oh! *This is a set!*' That was the kind of set he was used to in his own films. He liked the intimacy."

After the motel scene, Spielberg revisited three sequences he felt required additional close-ups and angles. Richard Dreyfuss found himself back behind the wheel of his power company truck for pickup shots of his first encounter at the railroad crossing, and Melinda Dillon spent another day crouched at the doggy door of the Guiler farmhouse, playing tug-of-war with the aliens for possession of Cary Guffey. Outside, on the airfield, Spielberg had a limousine parked next to a hangar in order to reshoot the first meeting between Lacombe and Laughlin.

At a nearby Mobile bank, one new scene was filmed before the crew resumed work on the Big Set: the meeting between Air Force official Major Benchley and the crowd who had been at Crescendo Summit on the night of Roy's first encounter. The sequence featured dozens of extras dressed as Air Force officials and television crews, all crammed into the set to add a sense of chaos to the event.

Before shooting the scene, Spielberg asked screenwriters Robert Zemeckis and Bob Gale to give the script pages a polish. The writing partners had been in Mobile for some time, working with Spielberg on the script for the director's next project, the World War II home-front comedy *1941*. Over the course of the two days at that location, Gale and Zemeckis met actor George DiCenzo, who was portraying Major Benchley. Several years later, when Zemeckis was directing *Back to the Future*, with Gale cowriting and producing, the duo remembered DiCenzo, and cast him as the father of Lea Thompson's character, Lorraine Baines.

With the meeting scene in the can, it was time to return to the Big Set to film the grand finale. The Mothership was landing.

ABOVE A bank in Mobile was used to shoot the scene of the Air Force officials meeting with locals who had experienced close encounters.

BELOW Joe Alves built a small motel room set in a corner of the hangar for the scene where Jillian discovers the location of Devils Tower.

OPPOSITE Roy Neary's power company truck was driven into the hangar, where additional shots for his encounter at the railroad crossing were filmed.

WELCOME TO EARTH

After the crew temporarily vacated the Box Canyon set, Joe Alves and his team worked nonstop to prepare for the arrival of the ETs. The live-action elements of the Mothership landing sequence would involve the culmination of months of behind-the-scenes work, and would prove to be the most difficult of the entire shoot. "It was a long, sustained series of challenges and problem-solving," remembers Spielberg.

When the time came to build the Mothership set, the overall design for the spacecraft had yet to be determined, although Alves had created several concept illustrations. Since a full-scale model of the Mothership was not necessary, or practical, for shooting on set, the production only had to design and build the lower part of the ship, from which the actors playing the aliens and abductees would emerge.

Without an overall blueprint to work from, Alves had a certain amount of freedom when designing the lower section of the Mothership. One night, while staring at the work lamp attached to his desk, he hit upon a suitably otherworldly idea that would form one of the central design elements of his set. He positioned

the lamp with its shade flat on the desk, and when he lifted the edge just a sliver, a bright beam of light shot out. He demonstrated the effect for Spielberg, who agreed that a similar effect would be the perfect way to frame the figures emerging from the underside of the ship.

With this effect in mind, Alves designed an enormous trapezoidal box measuring 80 feet long, which, in the scene, would be lowered to the stage floor before a ramp would open on its underside, emitting the brilliant light from within. The hatch was outfitted with hundreds of lights and mirrors, supplemented by additional arc lights, which would dazzle the cameras and obscure the figures appearing at the top of the ramp,

creating an air of anticipation and mystery. The ramp itself was covered with a reflective Mylar surface, and the stage was filled with smoke to further diffuse the images.

The set itself had to be engineered to move up and down in a precise straight line, to make sure it wouldn't sway or move in any unintended way. This was crucial for Douglas Trumbull and his visual effects crew, who would be adding animation to the exterior of the hatch and seamlessly joining the live-action footage to the Mothership visual effects. To that end, the exterior of the structure was draped in black velvet, which would help Trumbull's team create a perfect blend of live action and visual effects, using the black areas as a visual bridge between the two types of footage. The set would also need to support the weight of the two-dozen actors who would be filmed emerging from the ship. To ensure that it was sturdy enough to take

the weight, Alves used steel girders to construct this set, rather than the wood that would be used on a traditional build. The resulting shell weighed a staggering forty thousand pounds.

Roy Arbogast was responsible for the mechanical lowering of the massive set-piece structure, and his original plan was to have cranes on each side of it, moving the entire structure in perfect synchronicity. One of the local crew members came to him with a better idea, which would involve creating a hole in the roof of the hangar and using a 250-ton crane situated outside the building to raise and lower the Mothership structure and its boarding ramp. Arbogast eagerly agreed to the alternative plan because it meant he would no longer have to find space on set for two unwieldy cranes or oversee a complex coordination effort between the two crane operators.

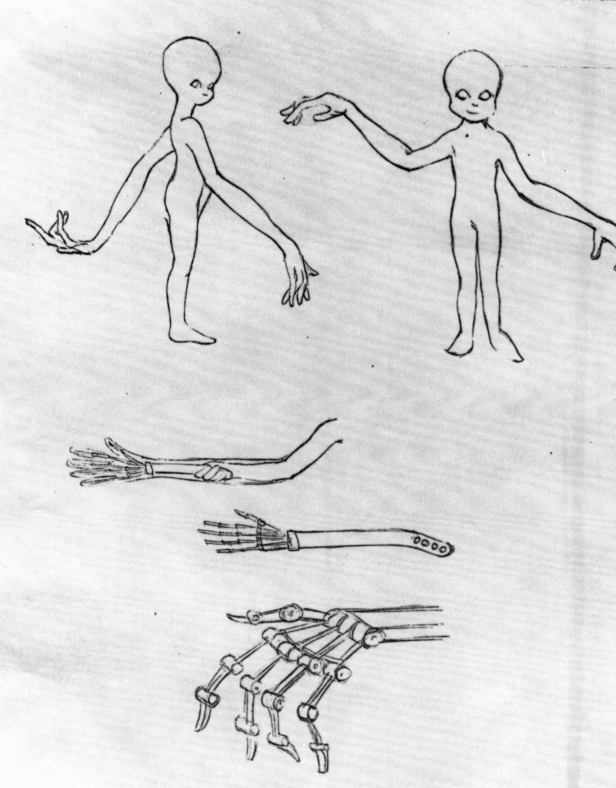

THE "GRAYS"

Spielberg had always intended to reveal the aliens in all their splendor at the end of *Close Encounters*, rather than just alluding to them and teasing the audience. Finding a look for the ETs that would be believable and also deliver the wow factor he needed for the film's finale was crucial.

OPPOSITE Based on the original concepts by Spielberg and Alves, the Burman company created costume and mask designs for the "Grays," including a proposal for articulated gloves that would be worn by the extras.

TOP One of the completed alien masks is used in an excised moment where Lacombe interacts with the ETs.

ABOVE Tom Burman (with beard) and David Ayres of the Burman Studios showcase the masks they created for the alien extras.

When designing the aliens, Spielberg and Joe Alves didn't set out to create wildly imaginative otherworldly beings. Instead, Spielberg was determined to keep the film as "factual" as possible, turning to the work of ufologist J. Allen Hynek as a starting point. In the majority of the credible reports Hynek had received regarding close encounters of the third kind, the descriptions of the ETs were remarkably similar: The beings, often known as "Grays," were nearly always described as being pale and diminutive, with large bulbous heads and two huge almond-shaped eyes. "That species was being reported all over the world," Spielberg says, "and that made me think there was some validity in the sightings."

Using the descriptions from Hynek's reports as a basis, Alves created a series of Gray sketches that authentically reproduced the main characteristics of the beings, as reported by witnesses. Makeup artist Frank Griffin was then brought onto the production to create physical alien masks based on Alves's designs. Brothers Tom and Ellis "Sonny" Burman, who specialized in special effects and monster makeup, were placed in charge of producing multiple versions of the masks based on Griffin's initial creations. The plan was to create two kinds of masks: One set, for close-up shots, would be fitted with animatronic mechanisms that could create a number of facial expressions, and the other set

would comprise non-articulated rubber masks for wide or longer shots involving the larger group of ETs. All the ET extras would also wear rubber alien hands with long, spindly fingers. It was originally planned that these gloves would allow the performers to pick up the earthlings' objects and equipment for examination, in order to highlight the beings' curiosity. An articulated prototype was designed but proved to be prohibitively expensive to produce, so Spielberg settled for a simpler, non-articulated glove.

To portray the ETs, Spielberg needed extras who were diminutive in stature and who possessed a similar body shape to the aliens described in Hynek's research. He decided to try casting a group of children, focusing in particular on girls ages six to seven, believing that they would display more natural grace than boys of the same age and size, and would be more open to direction. Realizing that boys would also be needed to wear the heavier articulated masks, Spielberg expanded the casting search to add five young males to the mix.

Casting agent Sally Dennison scoured the Mobile area, and found all her little extraterrestrials at a nearby ballet school. Actress/dancer Susan Heldfond was brought from Los Angeles to choreograph their movements following a recommendation from editor Verna Fields. Spielberg had a very specific vision for how the ETs should move, and for more

105

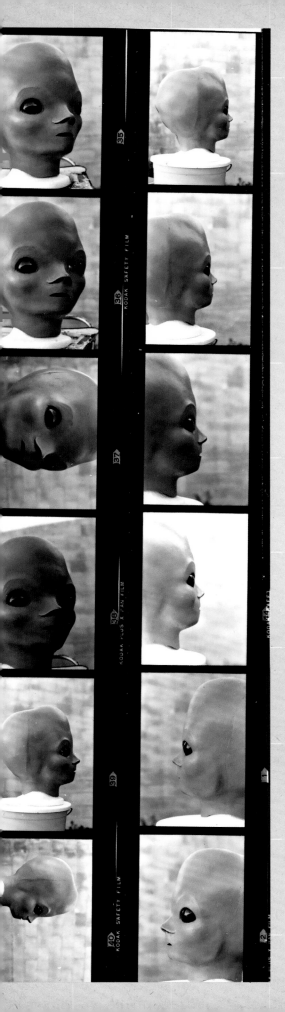

than a month before they stepped in front of the cameras, the children rehearsed their movements with Heldfond every day in a spare room at the hangar.

Before shooting, the Burmans outfitted the kids in simple leotards fitted with padding to give what Spielberg describes as "a different shape to the profile of the body." The leotards were also dyed to a monochromatic gray-blue to simulate the pale skin of the alien beings. Unfortunately, when the Burmans had first delivered the masks to Mobile, some of the girls found the heads so scary that they broke down in tears. Spielberg immediately ordered a redesign to create a softer look based on one of Alves's earlier designs. While they waited for the redesigned masks to arrive, the kids did get accustomed enough to the scarier originals to use them while practicing for the shoot. Because the masks had not been customized for each performer, however, some of the girls had trouble seeing out of the eyeholes, causing them to bump into one another during the rehearsals.

While the young performers rehearsed their alien choreography, stunt coordinator Buddy Joe Hooker worked with a group of mimes hired to play Box Canyon technicians. Spielberg wanted the mimes to move toward the Mothership in slow motion, while the children in the ET suits would move at a normal pace, thereby giving the sense that the aliens were moving much faster than the humans when the film was sped up in postproduction. The scene, which was to be shot at a reduced rate of twelve frames per second as opposed

to the standard twenty-four, was a hugely ambitious conception that would prove to be very problematic during filming.

In addition to working with the mimes, Hooker selected nine of the ET girls and gave them special training in wire work for a scene conceived by Spielberg that would see some of the aliens fly out of the Mothership and into the air while their counterparts scurried down the boarding ramp. Roy Arbogast fitted the chosen few with harnesses, and Hooker instructed them in the intricacies of being able to move naturally through the air.

OPPOSITE AND ABOVE Photo tests of the alien masks and a completed alien ready for filming.

BELOW Lacombe makes "contact" with one of the ETs.

THE RETURNEES (AUGUST 5–18, 1976)

The first sequence shot on the Mothership set saw Alves's structure successfully lowered to the ground using the industrial crane; the ship's ramp also descended to ground level with the ease and precision needed for the scene.

The crew then moved on to the musical communication scenes that would become a deeply iconic element of *Close Encounters'* cinematic legacy. As the cameras rolled, Phil Dodds, who had been hired for his proficiency with the ARP 2500 being used in the film,

finally got his close-up, expertly striking the synthesizer's keys in sync with a recording of the five-note theme that John Williams had made in preproduction.

Williams had used a synthesizer to create the music for the first contact sequence, with

one notable exception. Although the synthesizer was programmed with a tuba sound, when it came to the Mothership repeating the five-note combination, he wanted to strongly emphasize the thunderous last note. "We decided that a real tuba would be more of an arresting sound or noise," recalls Williams, "so it's a human blast of sound, rather than a machine, at the end, and it also has some oboe in it."

In the filming itself, that tuba blast was the cue for a glass window in one of the elevated cubicles to shatter, an unforgettable

ABOVE A George Jensen illustration shows the Mothership's hatch opening as scientists observe in awe.

moment that was particularly difficult to achieve. Arbogast was in charge of having the large panes of breakaway glass lifted into place with a crane for each take. Then, on cue, he would trigger an air cannon, which blew out the window. He'd then begin the process again, until Spielberg was happy with the shot. The director knew the importance and impact of that moment, and offered to personally pay for more panes of breakaway glass so he would be able to shoot more takes than were budgeted. The whole sequence was

particularly challenging for Vilmos Zsigmond, who couldn't pre-light the scene because his lights were so hot that they would begin to melt the glass. Once the lights were installed, the cinematographer had precious little time to make adjustments before the cameras rolled.

When it was time to shoot the abductees descending the ramp from the Mothership, Vilmos Zsigmond's lights flooded the hangar, beams bouncing off the reflective floor, as shadowy figures began to make their way through the dense fog. In the script, the

"returnees" included people from all walks of life, including the Navy pilots of Flight 19 who had vanished over the Bermuda Triangle in 1945. A total of twenty-four extras were chosen for the scene and dressed in period costume. Although they were not specifically identified onscreen, Spielberg dressed two other extras to represent a pair of historical figures noted for their disappearances in the

TOP LEFT Concept art by George Jensen of the returnees being met by Lacombe.

ABOVE In the final realization of the returnee sequence, an abducted pilot (Randy Herman) reports to Lacombe.

TOP RIGHT Hal Barwood (far right) appears as one of the returnee pilots.

CENTER RIGHT Concept art by George Jensen shows the returnees being checked off against a board of photographs of missing persons believed to have been abducted by UFOs.

OPPOSITE TOP The returnees disembark from the Mothership, silhouetted by the lighting effects inspired by Joe Alves's desk lamp.

OPPOSITE BOTTOM Spielberg mans a mobile camera rig to get additional shots of the action.

1930s—New York Supreme Court Justice Joseph Crater, and famed aviator Amelia Earhart.

Two of the first abductees to disembark were played by screenwriters Matthew Robbins and Hal Barwood, who had been brought to Mobile by Spielberg to do some last-minute revisions to the script. Robbins would also be pressed into service to direct a number of second unit shots. "Hal and I were working in our trailer one day," recalls Robbins, "and Steven stuck his head in the door and said, 'You guys want to be in the movie? Shave your beards off and put on uniforms, and you can be extras in the return of the pilots.'" The two enthusiastically went under the shears and quickly got fitted for costumes. "We made up names [for our characters] based on our wives," continues Robbins, "Hal became Harry Ward Craig, because his wife is Barbara Ward, and I became Matthew McMichael, because my wife was Janet McMichael." When it came time to walk out of the ship, one final adjustment needed to be made. The ramp itself was somewhat steep, and

the sleek Mylar surface, designed to bounce beams of light through the set, was slippery. "In order for us to get down that thing without falling on our asses, we had to have this kind of rubber cement on the soles of our shoes," explains Barwood. "The grips would come and slather it on. It would last about as long as you got down to the last yard or so, and then [because of the intense heat from the lights] it was peeling off the bottom [of our shoes]."

Multiple takes were ultimately required to capture the scene. As a result, the amount of time between the extras being loaded into the Mothership and the start of the scene had to be as brief as possible. The small compartment was oven-hot and became increasingly unbearable with each additional moment spent inside.

J. Allen Hynek also made a special appearance in the Mothership scene, having been invited to the set for a brief cameo as one of the scientists who watch the returnees disembark. Additionally, the sequence featured a cameo from Spielberg's cocker spaniel, Elmer, who happily trotted down the ramp past Cary Guffey and off camera to his waiting owner. Elmer was a regular fixture in Spielberg productions throughout the 1970s, also appearing in *The Sugarland Express*, *Jaws*, and *1941*.

Until *Close Encounters*, François Truffaut had not acted in another director's feature film, and one of the reasons he took the role was to get a better understanding of the filmmaking process from an actor's perspective. As might be expected, the experience of being directed rather than calling all the shots was an eye-opener for Truffaut. In one of the most notable lines in the returnee sequence, a scientist proclaims, "Einstein was right," awed by the fact that the abductees have not aged, despite having been away from Earth for many

years in some cases. The line had originally been written for Truffaut, but the French film-maker worried that his thick accent might make it sound unintentionally funny. Truffaut had fixated on this line for months, and shared his concerns with Bob Balaban. On the day, recalls Balaban, Truffaut was especially nervous and had prepared several excuses that he intended to use to avoid having to say the line. During the rehearsal of the scene, the issue became a moot point when Spielberg arbitrarily assigned the line to actor J. Patrick McNamara, who was playing one of the team leaders. Rather than being relieved, however, an indignant Truffaut sought out Balaban to ask, "Why has he given someone else *my* line?"

Although Truffaut very much enjoyed working with Spielberg on *Close Encounters*, he would never again act for another director, preferring to focus on his own directorial projects.

MEET THE ALIENS

Having completed shooting on the scenes of the abductees returning home, the production turned to one of the most daunting tasks of the entire schedule: the introduction of the aliens. One of the biggest concerns was the welfare of the children who would play the ETs. With long, arduous days of filming ahead, the production wanted to make sure the young performers were as comfortable as possible. As such, a note was attached to the call sheet each morning, alerting all departments to the correct protocol when filming with the youngsters: "Due to the physical difficulties in ET makeup, etc., it is imperative that once the children come on the set, we roll immediately. ADs (assistant directors) will not bring children in unless we can shoot immediately."

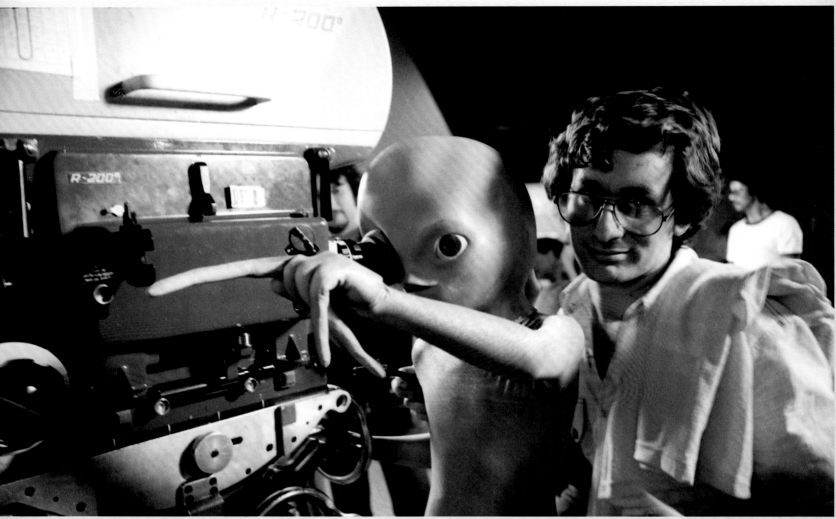

To facilitate these instructions, the process of preparing the children to shoot had to run like clockwork. Prior to filming, the fifty children would arrive on set and half their number would head to the wardrobe department, where they were dressed in the body stockings and alien gloves. After the remainder went through the same procedure, all fifty were moved to the hangar cafeteria to wait for the crew to finish their last-minute adjustments. When the cameras were ready to roll, the head appliances were attached, and the aliens were rushed to the set. Arriving in the compartment from which they would emerge on set, the kids were cooled by air conditioning installed by Joe Alves that offset the extreme heat generated by the lights in the unit.

While wrangling the ground-based aliens presented no significant problems, the flying aliens were another matter. Spielberg had ambitious plans for the flying sequence and even wanted the spectators to also take to the air. "I wrote in the script that there was a zero-gravity zone, right around the threshold of the Mothership," explains the director. "We were going to fly all of the technicians, with their spectrometers and Geiger counters and other devices. As they approach the Mothership, the ramp opens, and they were going to get into that zone and all start to float around. Having established that, I would then have the little Grays come out of the Mothership, and they were going to fly around the entire area and freak everybody out."

The plan was that when the hatch on the Mothership opened, the bulk of the aliens would proceed down the ramp, while the mimes playing technicians moved in slow motion around them. When they reached the

TOP Spielberg breaks in a new member of the camera crew.

ABOVE AND OPPOSITE The young girls portraying the aliens relax between takes.

112

WIRED

TUMBLING, TWIRLING

A

B

A & B SHOT SEPERATELY
FOR DIFFERENT SPEED.
MOVING FASTER —

end of the ramp, the nine flying aliens would rise out of the ship, soaring over the heads of the terrestrials.

The children playing the airborne ETs had their harnesses hooked onto wires and were loaded into the compartment ready to spring into the sky. The flying started out well, but after their first few flights, the girls on the wires began to get restless when they were lowered to the ground between takes. When standing, they were given enough slack to be comfortable, but couldn't venture very far beyond their landing spots. In order to get more room to maneuver, the girls would let themselves fall until they were lying flat on the ground, knowing that the rope operators couldn't see them through the smoke on the set. The rope operators would then give them the extra slack they needed to move more freely. "The girls figured out that they wanted to have more room so they could play,"

says physical effects technician Kevin Pike. "They had four more feet of freedom!"

Another problem arose when an unforeseen design flaw in the costumes caused delays in shooting. The body stockings had no seams, zippers, or trap doors, so when the girls had to use the restroom, it would take additional time to get them out of the suits and back in again.

Regardless of these practical issues, Spielberg soon discovered that the flying sequence was just not working. Watching dailies, he found that the slow-motion movement of the mimes did not look natural when it was sped up on film, and the aliens, both on the ground and in the air, took on a jerky quality in contrast. Rather than continue, Spielberg decided to drop the whole scene. "It just became too complicated, and I was already behind schedule," he says. "I realized if I shot that [entire] sequence I would be even further behind, so I discontinued it."

THESE PAGES Preproduction art by George Jensen illustrates Spielberg's original concept for an antigravity field that would surround the Mothership and allow the ETs to fly, with the technicians close to the ship also affected.

PAGES 116–117 A number of the alien extras were suspended by wires for the flying scene, but Spielberg later dropped the entire sequence.

PAGE 117, BOTTOM RIGHT UFO expert J. Allen Hynek finally gets to meet a group of "aliens."

 AS THE HUMANOIDS FAN OUT IN
ALL DIRECTIONS-
FLYING, RUNNING
GLIDING -

 THE TECHNICIANS SCATTER.

WHAT ARE WE LOOKING AT?

In the many weeks it would take to film *Close Encounters'* final thirty minutes, the actors spent a great deal of time looking skyward and reacting to an imaginary spacecraft. Although Spielberg was able to show his cast the conceptual art for the proposed Mothership designs, as well as the film's detailed storyboards, the images were a far cry from the visual splendor of the finished visual effects sequences.

To help his actors get a feel for the spectacle he planned to add to the film in postproduction, Spielberg walked each of them through the Mothership sequence, giving insights into how their characters would react to the arrival of the spacecraft. He suggested to Bob Balaban that his character was a cool, analytical type who begins the encounter tentatively but, over the course of the experience, gives in to his feelings of wonder. Conversely, Spielberg wanted François Truffaut's Lacombe to be enchanted with the visitors at all stages of the film's finale, believing that the audience's feelings about the extraterrestrials would be

ABOVE Production artwork is merged with footage filmed onstage to provide a preview of a finished Mothership shot.

largely determined by Lacombe's reactions. Knowing of Truffaut's affinity for kids, Spielberg suggested the Frenchman think of the aliens as children, a piece of direction that wouldn't involve a huge leap of faith given that the ETs were all seven years old or younger.

Melinda Dillon also received some choice direction from Spielberg during the scene where the Mothership arrives overhead and Jillian reacts with awe. "Steven says, 'I want you to hear, there's going to be a sound,'" she says. "'And then turn around, and then look up and see the person that you love the most

in the world.' So I turn around, and I see my grandmother. She had [recently] died, and I see her up there, huge, that big beautiful woman. My line was 'Oh my God!' and I barely, barely say it. I just kind of whispered it."

As the shooting in Box Canyon progressed, the long hours and excessive heat took its toll, prompting a number of the extras (including some of the children hired to play aliens) to leave the production. As a result, ADs Chuck Myers and Jim Bloom had to scramble to find replacements. If none were forthcoming, they had to shuffle the remaining extras into

119

OPPOSITE The cast members were each given specific direction on how their characters would react to the arrival of the UFOs.

ABOVE Spielberg lets off some steam with a stethoscope prop borrowed from one of the scientist extras.

positions that would keep the background filled. To his credit, Norman Dreyfuss had endured the sometimes trying conditions and stayed for the entire filming experience, although he admitted that his son had been right about how grueling the shoot would be.

For the remaining scenes on the Mothership set, Spielberg needed all the ETs he could get. For one scene in particular, Richard Dreyfuss donned a red jumpsuit and joined a group of characters known as "the pilgrims," humans who had volunteered to leave Earth with the aliens. Although Spielberg filmed the pilgrims walking up the ramp into the ship, he later decided not to use that shot. "I shot all the red-jumpsuited

people walking up the ramp, but I decided to cut that out, and only focus all my attention on [the aliens'] acceptance of Roy Neary," he says.

One of the most important scenes shot on the Mothership set showed Lacombe communicating with one of the ETs using the Kodály hand signals. Unfortunately, when the performer wearing the alien glove tried to replicate the hand movements, large creases were visible in the rubber. The sequence was completed, but Spielberg knew he would have to address the problem in postproduction.

When it was time to film Cary Guffey's reaction to the aliens' farewell, Spielberg took the boy aside for a chat. "This is one of the strongest memories that I have, because it was an emotional memory," remembers Guffey. "Steven came to me, and he said, 'You've gotta be upset now because your friends are going away. They're leaving you behind.' And in my four-year-old brain, what I understood him telling me was not that the aliens were going away, but that I was never going to get to go back to Douglas Preschool again, and see my friends, Mark and Donald, and the kids that I played with in the neighborhood. I was very upset, and I started to cry, which made Melinda Dillon cry, and which made everyone else on set start crying. There was no acting to it, it was me not understanding that what he was really telling me was 'The aliens are going away, these are your friends that we're talking about.' I thought he meant my real friends."

Richard Dreyfuss believes that it was ultimately Spielberg's talent for bringing together the perfect ensemble cast that made the final scenes of *Close Encounters of the Third Kind* so emotional and filled with wonder. "He hired masses of people for that final scene who all shared a certain ability of awe, of wonder, of terror, or fright, of being able to look off and freak out," he says. "I would say to Steven, in front of the team, in front of the camera, 'The name of the book that I will never write is *Steven, Have They Figured Out What I'm Looking Up in Awe At?*'"

The end of shooting on the Box Canyon set would be a wrap for Truffaut and Balaban (until they were needed for additional scenes back in Los Angeles and India). The night before he was scheduled to wrap, Truffaut invited the cast and crew to a party. The call sheet read:

Attention! Stand Up!! In order to say goodbye and thanks to this terrific crew & cast, I invite you to a party. It will be, I hope, a nice party.

François Truffaut, "The Frenchman"

STOP AND BE FRIENDLY

CRESCENDO SUMMIT (AUGUST 19–SEPTEMBER 2, 1976)

With two weeks left in the schedule, the production shifted to the adjacent hangar, where Alves had built two sets that would be used for the remainder of the shoot. The first of the sets was for Crescendo Summit, the curved stretch of cliffside roadway overlooking the Indiana countryside where Roy first meets Jillian and Barry, as well as several other UFO enthusiasts. Meanwhile, the other location, known on set as the "Notch," was a small segment at the top of Devils Tower where Roy and Jillian emerge after having escaped the military. From this vantage point, they have their first glimpse of the Project Mayflower proceedings down below.

These sets, like Box Canyon next door, were exteriors in the context of the story but were housed indoors so as not to leave the company at the mercy of the weather. Shooting them in a studio also allowed for total control of the lighting and other elements, factors very important when attempting to seamlessly add visual effects to live-action footage.

The Notch proved to be a fairly simple build and was constructed from the same fiberglass rocks that had lined the Box Canyon set. Crescendo Summit required a much more intricate design, however, involving a realistic-looking forest on one side of the hill and a curved road with a view of the Indiana countryside below and the sky above, both of which would be added using the visual effects technique of front projection. On the hillside portion of the set, Alves had planted a section of forest, replete with tall trees and dense foliage. While the extreme heat and humidity on the set was uncomfortable for the cast and crew, it proved perfect for cultivating the flora he had planted, which continued to grow at a healthy rate throughout the production's time in the hangar.

The road that went through the middle of the Crescendo Summit set would be used for a segment of the car chase in which the Indiana police, closely followed by Neary in his truck, engage in a breakneck pursuit of the three UFO scout ships. The size of the hangar, although smaller than that used for the Big Set, allowed Alves to build the road from one side of the building to the other, so that when he opened the hangar doors the vehicles could speed through the set at forty to fifty miles per hour. These driving shots would all be filmed after sundown, so the hangar doors could be left open without sunlight invading the set.

OPPOSITE TOP Melinda Dillon and Cary Guffey on the Crescendo Summit set. A combination of special effects elements, including matte paintings and front projection, were used to create the illusion that the actors were at a real outdoor location.

OPPOSITE BOTTOM LEFT Actor Roberts Blossom portrays one of the UFO enthusiasts who gather at the summit.

LEFT Roy makes the acquaintance of Jillian and her son.

TOP RIGHT Barry Guiler creates a familiar mud pie sculpture.

Crescendo Summit would be the first location in which Trumbull would use a specially built front projection unit, which could add certain pre-created visual effects elements to scenes as they were being shot. To facilitate the process, Trumbull built the largest portable process screen ever, standing at 38 feet tall and 130 feet wide, onto which he would project animated background elements created in preproduction, including star-filled skies and the lights of the distant towns. The screen itself was made from a reflective cloth that had millions of tiny glass beads affixed to its surface. The visual effects image sent to the screen would be bounced back by those beads at a high level of brightness, creating a final composite image of unparalleled clarity. In contrast to rear projection—a staple technique of the motion picture industry accomplished by projecting a pre-filmed background from behind the performers onto a small translucent screen on the set—the images produced by front projection were a huge leap forward and had been used to great effect by Stanley Kubrick and Trumbull on *2001: A Space Odyssey*, and also on Trumbull's own film, *Silent Running*.

The screen was used in two different ways during shooting. For scenes that involved static visual effects images such as a vista of Muncie,

Indiana, at night, Trumbull would use front projection to add this element to the footage while filming. However, as the more complex visual effects, such as shots of the scout ship UFOs flying, had yet to be created, sometimes the screen would essentially act like a traditional bluescreen onto which visual effects would be added during the postproduction process.

The Crescendo Summit scenes would also require practical effects. In one memorable moment, the crowd eagerly await an encounter with UFOs only to discover, to their profound disappointment, that the lights they saw in the distance belong to two military helicopters. To create the helicopter downdraft effects that would blast the actors in the scene, Arbogast eschewed the industry standard practice of renting wind machines from studios in LA and instead bought two swamp boats from a local Alabama resident. After removing the fans from the boats, he mounted them on large, movable platforms and aimed them at the set. While they were powerful enough to blow the cast around, the fans didn't have enough power to make the trees in the mini forest sway, and so Arbogast and his crew attached ropes to the trees and pulled them back and forth.

One key moment in the summit sequence, when three scout ships pass over the heads of Dreyfuss and the other believers, proved to be a particular challenge for Trumbull. "We hadn't designed the UFOs nor the Mothership yet," he says, "and we didn't know what color they'd be, or how bright they'd be, and we didn't know how [the shadows of the actors should look under their lights]." Despite not having exact reference points for the UFO lights, they decided to create the beams using "these gigantic arc lights hung from a crane, [that] we would swing . . . over the set, so that the lights of the UFOs would be shining on Melinda Dillon and Rick Dreyfuss and the kid, and it would look like an actual moving light."

However, after carrying out a test, they quickly realized they would have to find a different method. "It turned out to be extremely dangerous," Trumbull says. "The crane operator was on the other side of the mountain, and couldn't see where the light was. There was a really good chance that someone would be seriously injured in the process, so that idea was abandoned for safety reasons." In the end, they settled for a more practical solution. "[We] ended up [using] nothing more complicated than the panning of arc lights from the rafters across the set as a source of light," Trumbull reveals. Spielberg chose the color of the lights that would bathe the actors, and later, in postproduction, the visual effects team would match the lights of the UFOs they designed to the lights captured on set.

In the script, when Neary first runs into Barry Guiler, he almost does so literally. Speeding down the road following the mysterious lights, Roy slams on the brakes when he sees Barry in the middle of the road at Crescendo Summit. Fortunately, Barry's mother snatches him out of the way, and, with the boy in her arms, rolls onto the hillside and away from traffic. Dreyfuss, Dillon, and Guffey would all be doubled by Buddy Joe Hooker's stunt team for the potentially dangerous shot, although the youngest member of the trio wanted in on the action. Watching the rehearsal, Guffey begged Spielberg to allow him to do the shot himself, but to no avail.

Although most of the work during the last two weeks in Alabama took place on the Crescendo Summit set, there were some necessary pickup shots to do on the Notch, first with Melinda Dillon and Richard Dreyfuss. Actor Josef Sommer was brought to Mobile to reprise his role as escapee Larry Butler and once again get gassed by the military.

Dreyfuss would take one more turn in his power company truck for an additional shot that would complete the railroad-crossing scene they had begun shooting when the company first moved to Mobile. In a corner of the hangar

BOTTOM LEFT The Crescendo Summit set was fully functional and allowed cars to drive through at a speed of 40 mph.

BELOW Special effects diagrams show the proposed movement of the saucers through the summit.

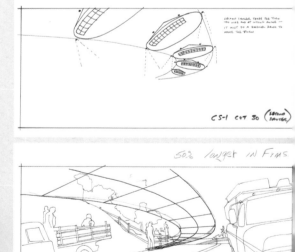

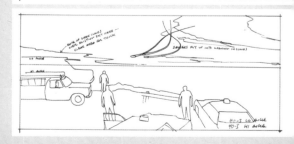

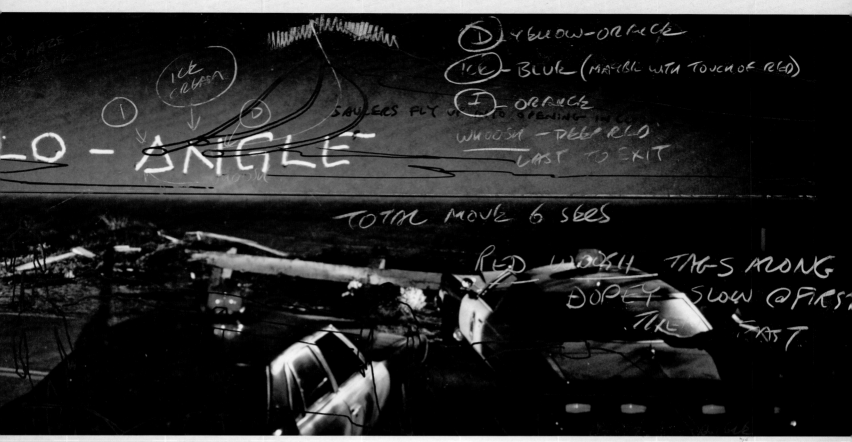

where Crescendo Summit was being shot, Arbogast's crew had set up the truck's cab, and mounted it on a gimbal that would allow the vehicle to spin 360 degrees. Moments before the camera (and the truck) started to roll with Dreyfuss in the driver's seat, prop master Sam Gordon brought out a bowl of glitter and spread it liberally all over the dashboard. Although it's not identifiable in the finished footage, the glitter interacted with cinematographer Vilmos Zsigmond's lighting in a dynamic way, giving the air a sparkling quality. "That's the great thing about movies," Dreyfuss says of the pickup shot. "It was so simple to do, and took no time at all. All Steven did was lock the camera onto the gimbal, and as they turned the truck, everything else went floating around. We did it twice, and that was it. It was easy, it was fun, and I knew when he told me about it what a showstopper it was going to be."

The last few days in Mobile were taken up with additional special effects shots as the team raced to get out of the hangars, under the watchful eyes of the studio, which was growing increasingly nervous about the film's budget and schedule. The hangars were cleared out, equipment returned and props put up for sale. A number of the fiberglass rocks from Box Canyon and the Notch were shipped to Los Angeles in case they would be needed for retakes, but the bulk of them proved a popular sale item for the Mobile locals. As Joe Alves had predicted, once the Neary house was cleaned up and returned to its original, pristine condition, Columbia Pictures was able to sell the property, which now had the added pedigree of being featured in a major motion picture, for a profit of $20,000.

While the production had remained on location two weeks longer than originally scheduled, the studio was still hopeful they could make their planned release date of Easter 1977.

TOP AND ABOVE To plan the police/UFO chase scene, Trumbull used a plastic overlay placed across still frames from the live-action footage to notate the paths of the spaceships as well as the color of their lights.

CENTER LEFT Producer Julia Phillips makes a cameo as one of the UFO watchers at Crescendo Summit.

BELOW Bob Balaban, who was not featured in the Crescendo Summit scenes, pays a visit to the location's impressive indoor set.

PART THREE

GOING "POST-AL"

Spielberg and company had returned to Los Angeles with the bulk of the live-action shooting completed, but there was still one big sequence outstanding which would require the production to travel to India. The scene would involve Lacombe and Laughlin observing the population of an Indian village chanting the iconic five notes, a sound Lacombe would record and later play back for his colleagues during his presentation in the auditorium scene. Originally scheduled for the end of September 1976, the scene was pushed back several times, mostly because of Truffaut's hectic schedule. The French auteur was premiering his film *Small Change* at the New York Film Festival in early October, and then was set to begin directing *L'Homme qui aimait les femmes* (*The Man Who Loved Women*), one of two projects he had written during his downtime on *Close Encounters*.

PAGES 126–127 George Jensen preproduction art shows the moment of truth as the scientists prepare to come face-to-face with extraterrestrials.

TOP AND ABOVE Spielberg reviews the cut scenes with editor Michael Kahn and his assistants.

OPPOSITE TOP Douglas Trumbull discusses a special effects shot with Spielberg.

OPPOSITE BOTTOM Spielberg makes use of some of the excess footage from the shoot.

During this period, Bob Balaban received several calls from producer Julia Phillips informing him of their intent to shoot in India imminently, only to then be told that filming was postponed. On two of those occasions he endured painful rounds of inoculations in preparation for trips that would be canceled and vowed not to go through a third round of injections until he had an airline ticket in hand. The production would not reach the subcontinent until February of 1977.

While waiting for the India shoot to be scheduled, there was more than enough postproduction work to keep the filmmakers fully occupied. Michael Kahn had begun the editing process during the shoot. In Mobile,

he worked from a large room in the house he shared with Spielberg so that they could collaborate on the edit whenever the director had spare time. During a visit to the editing room, François Truffaut had been astounded by the amount of footage, proclaiming it was enough for three or four of his own films. Kahn would subsequently return from Mobile with more than 250,000 feet of film and set up shop in a condominium in Marina del Rey, a seaside section of Los Angeles County.

Kahn's first order of business was to properly arrange all the scenes. "We took all these rolls of film and lined the entire floor of that huge apartment," he remembers. "Then we'd run the reels and we would mark down

what was on each reel. You'd walk in there, and you're dodging footage, it was all over the floor." The large amount of film that Spielberg had shot on location was not a sign of excess, however, but an important part of the director's process. "He wanted to have enough options so we could do what he wanted later," says Kahn. "He wants to be sure he can still be directing the film after he's done shooting it."

Meanwhile, before the start of production, Douglas Trumbull had rented out a large facility in Marina del Rey, just a block from the offices of his visual effects house, Future General. The 13,500-square-foot warehouse was divided into dedicated sections for each of the *Close Encounters* visual effects departments, including the model makers, the optical effects department, the animators, and the matte painting team. There was also an area set aside for the filming of visual effects elements. Trumbull, his director of photography, Richard Yuricich, and their production manager, Robert Shepherd, had stocked the warehouse with 65mm cameras, lights, film processors, and many other pieces of equipment essential to the project. The facility was established before shooting started so that Trumbull could create the plates for front projection that would be needed during filming and also get a head start on some of the other visual effects elements before the main unit returned from Alabama.

The proximity of the editing room and the visual effects house was convenient for Spielberg, who could easily dart between the two locations to work with Kahn and Trumbull.

CLOUDY WITH A CHANCE OF ETS

Trumbull started his work with a visual effect that would become one of the most memorable elements of the finished film. During their conversations about the way the UFOs would make their grand entrance in several scenes, Spielberg had stated that he wanted to see them emerge from banks of billowing clouds. Trumbull loved the concept, as it was something he had briefly explored during his work on *2001: A Space Odyssey*. "[On Kubrick's film] we were experimenting with liquids in tanks for a whole astronomical sequence we called 'The Manhattan Project,'" he recalls. "One day we were putting cream in a cup of coffee, and we realized there were these really cool little miniature clouds forming inside the coffee, and we said, 'Let's get a little aquarium and some paints and dyes, and see what happens.' That never went anywhere on *2001*, but it was an idea in the back of my mind [and] it emerged again when Spielberg wanted clouds for *Close Encounters*."

Given his immense workload, Trumbull was unable to carry out the initial testing himself, and so turned to his new assistant, Scott Squires, a nineteen-year-old transplant from Indiana who had recently moved to California to find work in the visual effects industry. On his very first day on the job, Squires found himself researching one of the most important visual effects elements in the film. "Doug handed me a 20-gallon aquarium and $20 in petty cash," Squires recalls, "so I went off to the local grocery store, picked up a bunch of stuff, and started experimenting. By the end of the week, by trying things and then talking to very smart people in Doug's group, I came up with the answers."

In his trials, Squires discovered that gravity would need to play a key role in the execution of the effect. "The final mixture [involved] taking advantage of specific gravity by having saltwater as a bottom layer and freshwater on top, because the saltwater is heavier," he says. After filling the tank halfway with saltwater, Squires applied a very thin

Trumbull used a trigger-activated rod-like device to release the desired amount of paint into the tank wherever needed. The lights representing the UFOs were also created practically through use of a wand filled with fiber optics and fitted with a small light on its tip. The wand would be placed behind the paint cloud as it billowed in the tank and its light, which could also be made to flash, eerily illuminated the clouds. Spielberg was delighted with the initial screen test of the process, and Squires immediately went to work on producing the numerous shots that would be used in the film. "Once you did a set of clouds, to do the next take, you had to drain it [the tank], rinse it out, and then pump new water back in," he says. "You could only get two takes a day, typically."

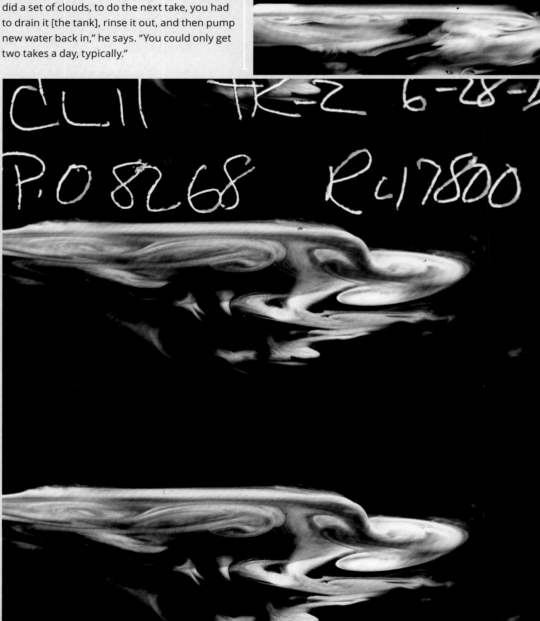

sheet of plastic, akin to a garbage bag, and then filled the remainder of the tank with freshwater. The plastic was carefully removed so that the liquids would remain separate. "We would inject white tempera paint into the top layer, and then it would billow out, just like the cream in your coffee," continues Squires. "Once it hit the saltwater layer, it would flatten out, just like a real cloud does because of air pressure and so forth. By filming at different frame rates and different angles, we could get the types of clouds we wanted."

THESE PAGES Test shots of the cloud formations.
ABOVE Trumbull and Richard Yuricich shoot with the cloud tank.

CLOUDS BUILD

ABOVE AND LEFT The special effects team used this sketch and overlay on a still frame to plan the clouds at the Guiler farm that herald the arrival of ETs.

RIGHT Additional formations created in the cloud tank.

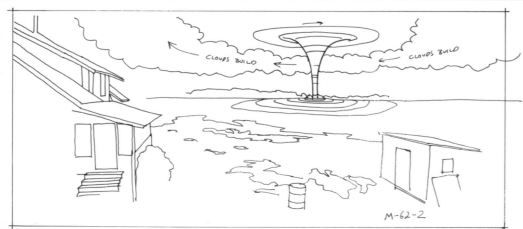

CLOUDS BUILD   CLOUDS BUILD

M-62-2

MATT'S MATTES

In preproduction, it was initially decided that traditional matte painting techniques—in which a detailed painting is superimposed onto live-action footage in postproduction to create the illusion that the scene has background elements not present during shooting—would not be used for scenes that required visual effects augmentation. Instead, the plan was to use a blend of pre-created animation elements plus footage of miniature spaceships and other elements that would be combined with live action on set using the front projection process. While Richard Yuricich thought it could be accomplished, he wanted to have a contingency plan. "We all thought that miniatures used in composites and photographed as front projection plates should handle all composite needs," he says, "but time restraints became an issue. . . . Building all of the flying devices early enough to be incorporated into front projection plates just wasn't going to happen."

When it indeed became clear that their plans for the visual effects were a little too ambitious, Yuricich brought in his older brother Matthew, a celebrated matte artist whose work had appeared in films including *North by Northwest, Ben-Hur, Mutiny on the Bounty, The Poseidon Adventure, Young Frankenstein, The Towering Inferno,* and 1973's *Westworld.* He won an Oscar for his much-lauded work on the 1976 futuristic sci-fi thriller *Logan's Run.* As is necessary in the art of matte painting, his work for *Close Encounters* would be so skilled and subtle that it was virtually impossible to detect where the live-action portion of a scene ended and the painted backgrounds began.

For the scene in which Roy and Jillian are perched on Devils Tower overlooking the Box Canyon complex, Matthew created more than twenty-five pieces, covering the various angles that Spielberg wanted to shoot. He also painted the surrounding forests and vistas that stretched out into the night, his paintings perfectly blending with the horseshoe-shaped canyon that was ringed with the rocks created by Joe Alves. The elder Yuricich also augmented Douglas Trumbull's 65mm footage of Melinda Dillon running back to the Guiler farmhouse when she sees the ominous clouds forming, adding the darkening skies, trees, and nearby farms.

THESE PAGES Greg Jein's miniature models of a rural landscape (foreground) are seamlessly blended with Matthew Yuricich's matte paintings to create stunningly realistic vistas.

PAGES 136–137 A George Jensen production illustration shows Roy and Jillian peering down on Box Canyon. The insets reveal how the final frame will be assembled using live-action footage and special effects plates.

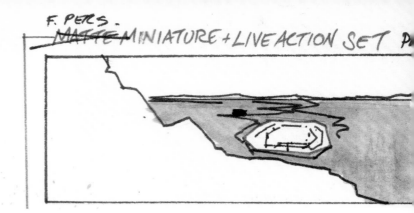

EFFECT #3   GREENHOUSE & JILLIAN OVERLOOKIN

SKY EFFECTS PLATE ✳

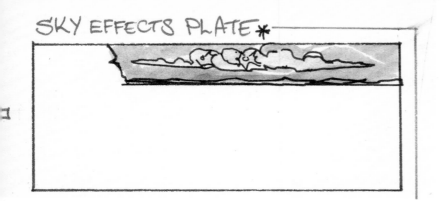

...ASE - CLOUDS MOVE - ESCORTED BY LIGHTS

Shortly after principal photography had been completed, and the postproduction work began in full force, Matthew Yuricich took on an apprentice. Eighteen-year-old Rocco Gioffre, an aspiring artist with an interest in film effects, was just out of high school in Lorain, Ohio, the hometown of the Yuricich brothers.

One of Gioffre's first big jobs was helping to create the matte paintings that would be used to show the UFO-related blackout in Muncie, Indiana. To create the moment, a wide-angle photograph of a Los Angeles neighborhood was taken from a high building in late afternoon, as the sun was just starting to set. The negative was then color corrected, making it seem as if the shot were taken at night, and projected onto a black board on a matte stand. Gioffre then hand-painted lights in the windows of every house in the photographed neighborhood. "We would roll on that shot

for two seconds before we started blinking any lights out," explains Gioffre. "They would stop the camera, because we were shooting in stop-motion speeds, and I'd walk into the matte stand area and blacken out a certain number of windows. We'd roll out a few more seconds, stop the camera again, and blacken out a few more windows." This would continue until the neighborhood, section by section, was totally blacked out.

Gioffre also assisted Matthew on some of the Box Canyon paintings, enhancing the glow of the stadium lights and the blue lights on the landing strip.

By the end of his time on the film, Matthew Yuricich, with Gioffre's help, would deliver more than one hundred separate works of art for *Close Encounters*, once again helping to create some of the most memorable vistas in motion picture history.

138

ABOVE Yuricich painted numerous versions of the area surrounding Box Canyon, extending the forest and the lights of the landing strip and adding the distant horizon.

RIGHT Frames from a "PTG test," in which the effects department photographs a matte painting combined with all other optical elements that will appear in the final shot.

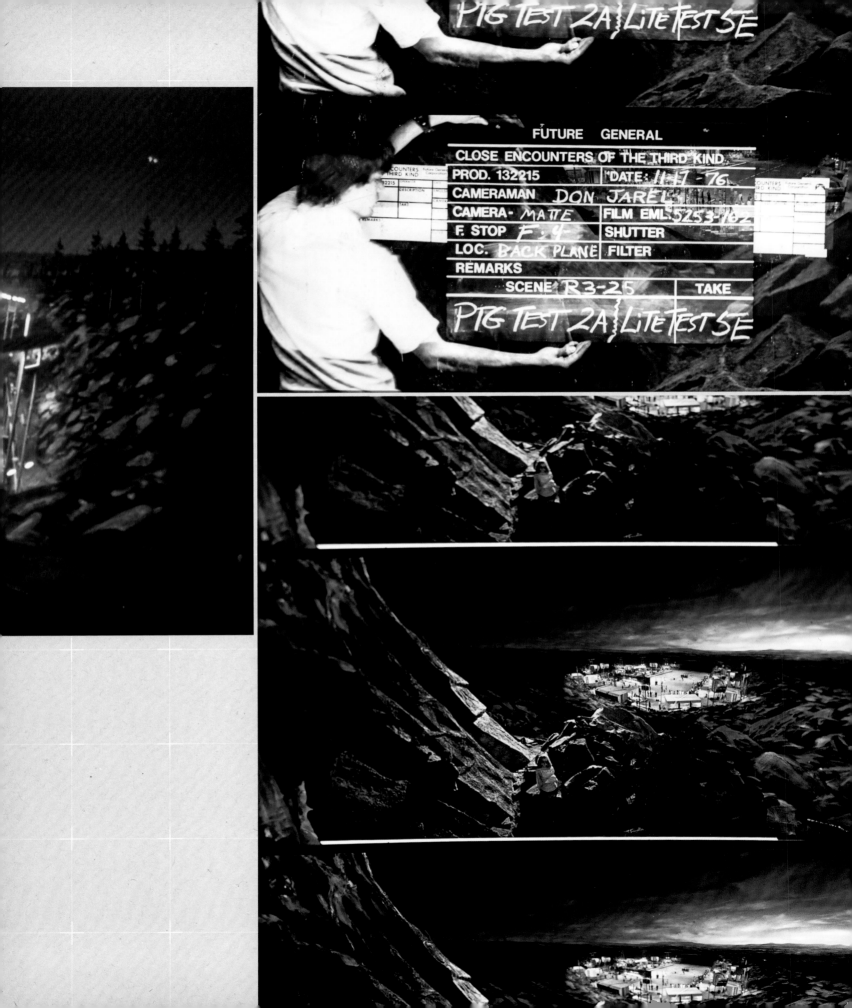

Additional matte paintings by Matthew Yuricich.

ABOVE This black-and-white Crescendo Summit matte board was used to prevent the live-action and front projection terrain images from bleeding into the lightning flash and cloud effects that would be added to the shot.

BELOW A matte used on the "Notch" segment of the set, enhancing the sky, trees, and rocks.

TOP RIGHT Matthew Yuricich's panorama of Devils Tower would ultimately go unused, as Douglas Trumbull and Richard Yuricich were able to get a perfect shot of the real butte just before leaving Wyoming.

BOTTOM RIGHT This matte painting was created mainly for the addition of the blue horizon glow and the brighter terrain area surrounding the live action of the Box Canyon complex. The silhouetted black area is where the Devils Tower miniature was added.

MODEL BEHAVIOR

Early in the preproduction process, Spielberg had reached out to another *2001: A Space Odyssey* alumnus, animator Colin Cantwell. Cantwell had been doing extensive work with computer graphics over the years and believed he could digitally animate the spaceships, as well as many of the other elements of the script. He was hired to do a test of three ships flying across the screen, but unfortunately it took weeks for Cantwell to finish the one shot, and the images were far from what Spielberg had in mind. It was then decided that *Close Encounters* would rely on miniature models, a time-honored practice with roots going back to the earliest days of film. The film's miniature work would mainly be focused on building the numerous UFO models needed, but it would include scale miniatures of a number of the sets as well.

TOP Gregory Jein puts the final touches on a miniature stretch of a rural road.

ABOVE AND BELOW Jein's first model for *Close Encounters* was a miniature version of Crescendo Summit and its immediate surroundings.

OPPOSITE The extended area around the miniature version of Crescendo Summit included a farmhouse, rural roadways, and a mini version of Neary's truck.

To lead his model-making team, Trumbull's production manager, Robert Shepherd, brought in Gregory Jein, who he'd worked with in the past and who had created impressive models for the low-budget 1974 sci-fi comedies *Flesh Gordon* and *Dark Star*. "It was only going to be a few weeks' work," Jein says with a laugh. "It went a little longer than that."

Those few weeks of work would extend to a total of eighteen months, with Jein and his team producing dozens of miniature pieces. His first project was a miniature of the Crescendo Summit set, complete with farmhouse, all of which would be filmed as a plate for front projection. Jein worked with artist Dan Goozeé, who had created pencil sketch storyboards of the Crescendo Summit scene, to design his miniature and determine its exact proportions. Their method involved projecting one of Goozeé's storyboards onto a flat surface, essentially like a camera slide, and then physically building the miniature around and within the black-and-white lines of his projected drawing.

Jein also used this method to create a miniature of the railroad crossing where Neary's work truck would be stalled. When he sent a Polaroid of the completed piece to Douglas Trumbull, who was on set in Mobile, he got a message back, saying, "Doug wants to know where you took that picture at, because that's exactly what they want." As a result, the production ended up using Jein's model as a basis for the real location, dressing it to look like the miniature so the two would match perfectly in postproduction.

Starting with a block of foam, Jein also sculpted a painstakingly detailed model of Devils Tower, along with the surrounding forestry and landscape. This model was intended for a shot where the Mothership rises into view over the top of the mountain, the camera viewing it from below. Additionally, Jein would be responsible for creating the Mothership model itself, although its final form wouldn't be determined until later in the production. Before then, Jein had to tackle the challenge of creating a miniature that would match a pickup shot that Spielberg filmed on December 1, 1976, while waiting for the India shoot to be confirmed. One of the remaining pieces the director needed to complete the police chase he had started filming in Mobile, the shot would focus on a police car racing past a tollbooth in pursuit of UFOs witnessed by Neary, before crashing through a barrier and coming to a stop at the bottom of a hill.

The tollbooth scene presented a major visual effects challenge in that it needed to be bathed with the passing lights of the UFOs, an effect that couldn't be achieved at a practical location without a huge amount of lighting and rigging that just would not be financially or logistically possible. To solve the issue and

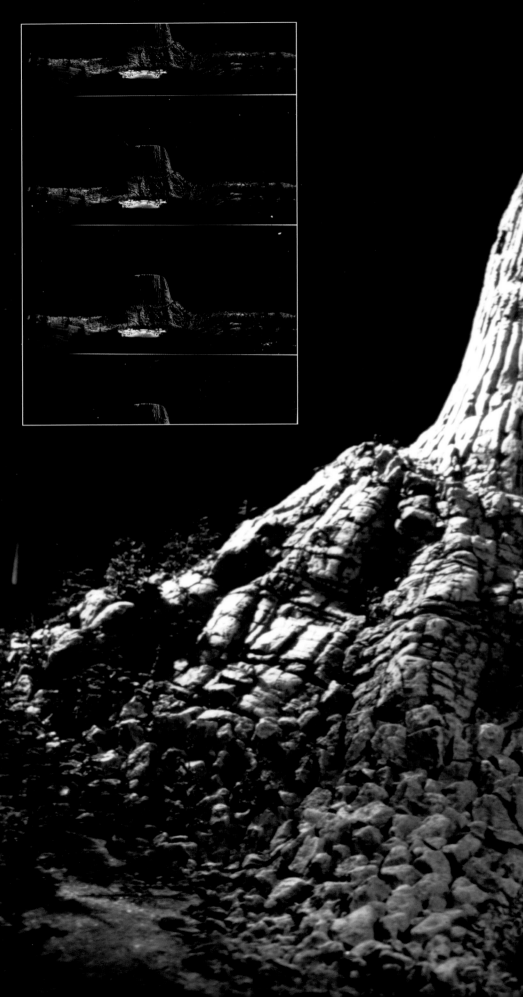

provide a version of the tollbooth that could be easily lit, Greg Jein created a perfect one-twelfth scale model of the tollbooth filmed on location as well as 8-inch versions of the saucers that would fly through the model on a track. The three UFO models were built out of vacuum-formed styrene plastic, along with plexiglass, aluminum, and wood, and took less than a week to assemble. Thanks to Jein's meticulous attention to detail, the footage of the miniature tollbooth later merged perfectly with the live-action car chase shots. Getting that live-action footage had proved to be more eventful than planned, however.

Filmed at a real tollbooth on the Vincent Thomas Bridge in San Pedro, California, the police car crash segment of the pickup shot required Joe Alves and Roy Arbogast's crews to build a stunt ramp at the location to the exact specifications of stunt coordinator Buddy Joe Hooker. Writers Bob Gale and Robert Zemeckis happened to visit the set that night, at the invitation of Spielberg, and witnessed the stunt being filmed. "He [Buddy Joe Hooker] said to the stunt double who would be driving the car, 'I've designed this so you have to hit the ramp at exactly 40 miles an hour, and if you do that, the car's going to land right [in the correct spot],'" recounts Gale. Unfortunately, the driver hit the ramp at a speed closer to 50 mph. "He overshot the mark," Gale continues. "He wrecked his car, because it went to the wrong place, smashing into something." Paramedics extracted the stuntman from the totaled vehicle and got him to a waiting ambulance. He suffered a concussion and some broken bones, but would make a full recovery. Despite the unfortunate outcome of the stunt, the footage itself was usable, and the take appeared in the final film.

TOP Jein was tasked with building an exact miniature of the tollbooth seen in the live-action footage of the UFO/police chase.

RIGHT A painstakingly detailed recreation of Devils Tower built by Jein.

TOP RIGHT (inset) Jein's model of Devils Tower was combined with a background matte and live-action footage of the landing site.

OPPOSITE TOP RIGHT (inset) Shooting the tabletop model of Devils Tower.

THESE PAGES In the small Indian village of Hal, Spielberg and company assembled thousands of extras to chant the five musical notes.

OPPOSITE TOP Truffaut on location in India.

A PASSAGE TO INDIA

After many postponements (and at least two sets of vaccinations), the cast and crew reassembled in Bombay (now Mumbai) on February 24, 1977, to begin two days of filming. The decision to film in India was partially determined by the fact that any box-office profits Columbia Pictures made from its films in the country could not be transferred to the United States and had to remain in India. Since the funds were confined to local banks, it made good financial sense to use the money for a location shoot rather than letting it lie dormant.

Vilmos Zsigmond had moved on to shoot Michael Cimino's *The Deer Hunter*, so Spielberg brought in British cinematographer Douglas Slocombe (*The Man in the White Suit*, *The Lavender Hill Mob*, *The Great Gatsby*) to replace him. Chuck Myers had also moved on to another film, so his second AD, Jim Bloom, received a "field promotion" to first AD.

The filming location was a small, isolated village called Hal, approximately forty miles from Mumbai, where the Indian production manager had assembled two thousand extras for the scene. The extreme heat and humidity in Hal was even more severe than in Mobile, and on the first day of shooting, both François Truffaut and Jim Bloom were stricken with heat exhaustion. After a brief respite, Truffaut was able to return to work, but Jim Bloom was not as lucky, and had to spend the rest of the shoot in his hotel.

The shooting was chaotic and slow. When a lunch break was called, a good number of the extras left to go to a local mosque to pray and were late returning. Meanwhile, an Indian choral leader hired to lead the extras in the chant of the five tones gave them the wrong notes, which they repeated over and over, despite the efforts of the production people to correct the error. The pivotal moment in which all the extras were to point to the sky, indicating where the five notes originated, took even more time, as several extras would point in the wrong direction, while others would lower their hands before Spielberg yelled "Cut!"

Though the India experience was not the most comfortable, the director got the scenes he needed and also, rather unexpectedly, came up with a winning idea for the design of the Mothership. As postproduction continued, Spielberg had grown less and less satisfied

147

THESE PAGES Production illustrator George Jensen's first drawings of the Mothership approaching Devils Tower.

PAGES 150–151 Ralph McQuarrie's illustration of the Mothership based on Spielberg's concept.

with the Mothership concepts he had been reviewing, feeling that none of them were as visually striking as the finale of *Close Encounters* demanded. One of the initial ideas that the director communicated to production designer Joe Alves was that the craft be football-shaped but with one flat end, almost like a clothes iron. He also wanted the ship to be so large that it blocked out the stars when hovering above those gathered at Box Canyon. While these starting points guided the design process in its early stages, the specifics of the Mothership design eluded Spielberg until a car ride between the location at Hal and the hotel back in Mumbai: "When we finished shooting at night, we would pass this huge oil refinery, and I thought, 'Oh my God, what if the entire bottom of the Mothership looked exactly like that?'"

In the final film, the city skyline–like bottom of the Mothership, inspired by the towers of the oil refinery, actually turns out to be the top of the ship when the craft flips over and lands on the dome side. It wasn't until Spielberg returned to Los Angeles that he realized how this dome portion of the ship should be designed.

"I remember being on Mulholland Drive," he recalls, "looking down at the San Fernando Valley, and thinking, 'And what if the entire dome . . . could look like the San Fernando Valley? All those lights at night!' That's where those two ideas were blended."

Spielberg shared his ideas with Ralph McQuarrie, an acclaimed illustrator who had just created a series of iconic concept designs for *Star Wars*. The artist deftly combined the Mumbai oil refinery and San Fernando Valley ideas into a stunning concept painting, delivering exactly the design Spielberg desired.

THE MOTHER OF ALL SHIPS

Guided by some original direction from Spielberg and Trumbull, Greg Jein and his team had almost completed a four-foot-high model of the Mothership as Spielberg was returning from India. "The original Mothership that we built was like a tepee cut in half, but glossy black," says Jein, "and we had just about finished when they said, 'We got a better design, scrap that.' We threw out the giant tepee."

Jein was given copies of McQuarrie's new design, using it as reference for building a seven-inch maquette. After seeing the preliminary miniature, Spielberg and Trumbull gave him the go-ahead to create a detailed model of the Mothership for filming. "The main thing on my agenda was to make sure [the model] . . . wasn't too hard-edged and shiny, which would give away the scale," explains the model builder. "We had a lot of refractive areas on it and a lot of shadowy areas on it, kind of like looking at a Seurat painting compared to a Rembrandt. A lot of dots instead of hard edges."

When constructing the model, Jein started from the dome segment at the bottom of the ship, and worked his way up. The base upon which the rest of the Mothership would sit was a brown acrylic bowl (salvaged from his "tepee"), to which Jein added surface detail for texture. "We decided we didn't have enough time to build the whole ship all the way around,

so let's just build a quarter of it, make a mold, and then put all the pieces together so the basic substructure would be there," he says.

Once the team had the form assembled, they started to create the skyscraper-like structures for the top of the ship. The cylinders themselves were little aluminum tubes that came from a supplier of structural pieces for architectural models. More materials for decorating the ship's upper half came from a nearby model train store—including railroad towers, semaphores, and more. In addition to the aluminum tubes, the team produced other structures and spires for the city in the sky. "The basic patterns [for the structures] were made out of wood, and we fiberglassed them and drilled zillions of holes in them [as they had for the aluminum tubes], and we put miles of fiber optics into the holes," says Jein. "Anybody who wasn't doing anything was [enlisted to drill] holes in the tubes for the [fiber optics] to go

TOP AND OPPOSITE Additional Mothership concept paintings by Ralph McQuarrie.

ABOVE Jein and his team begin the construction of the Mothership.

PAGES 154–155 The Mothership model is constructed and filmed. The model was incredibly detailed and included a number of in-jokes, including a tiny R2-D2 (bottom right).

PAGES 156–157 Beauty shots of the final Mothership model. The lights are a result of hundreds of bulbs illuminating the thousands of hand-drilled holes in the model's components.

(Continued on page 161)

152

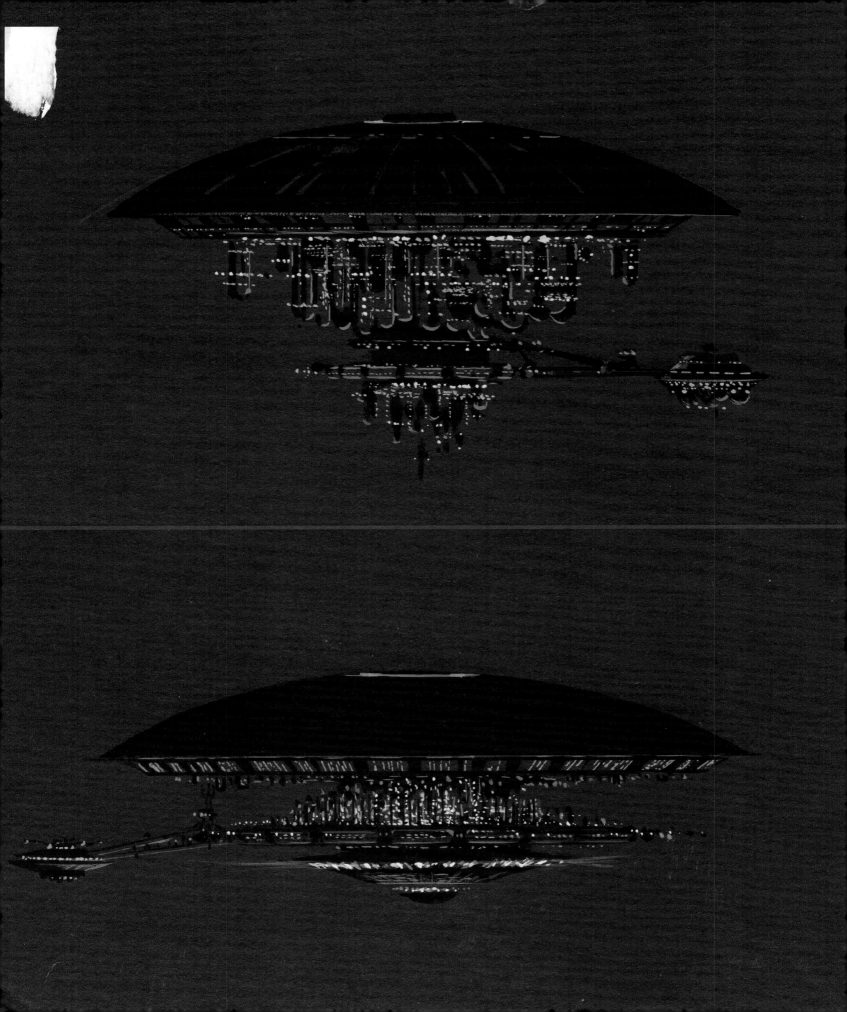

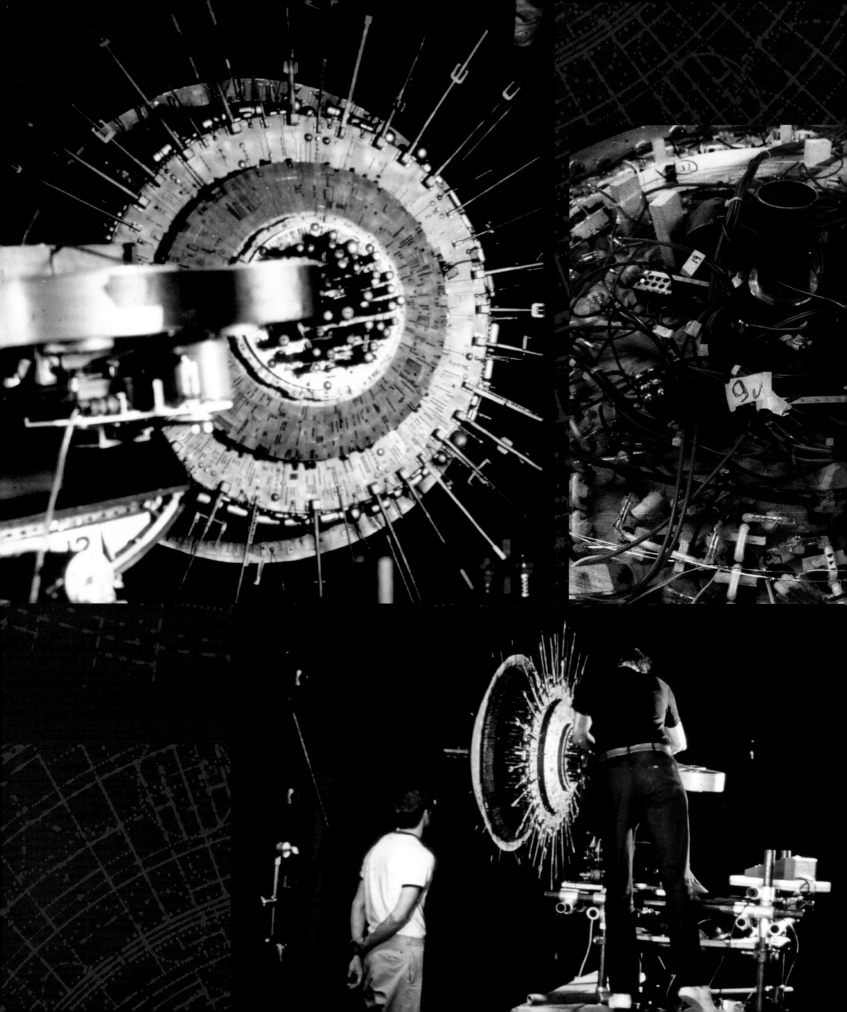

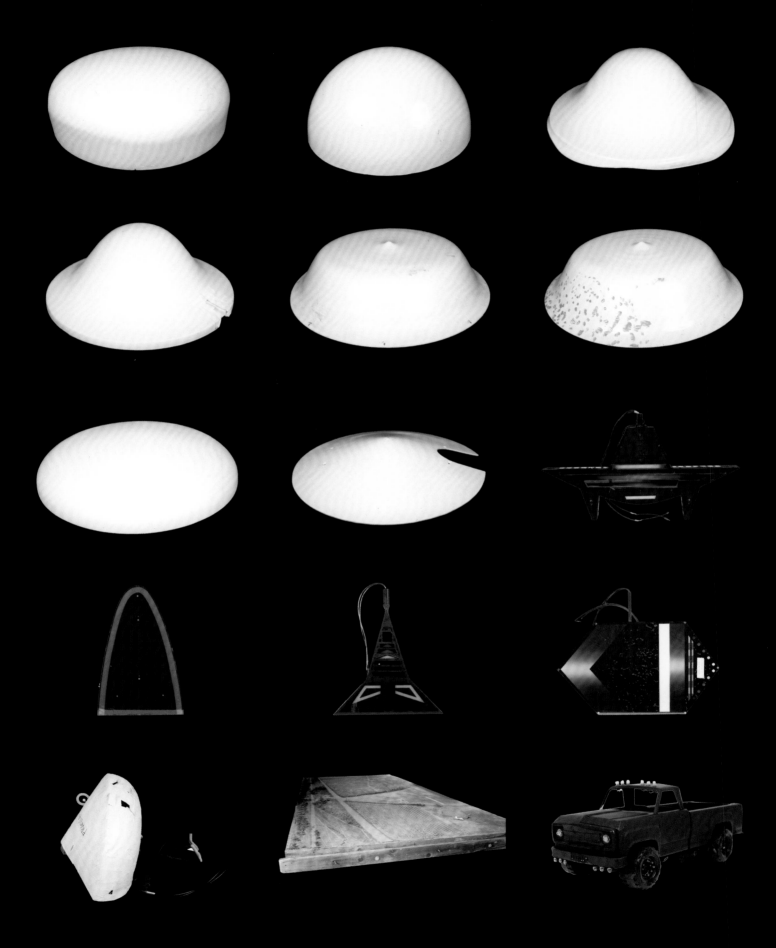

1.

A SLIVER OF WHITE LIGHT
APPROACHES..

2.

FILLING THE SCREEN — THE
GAPING MOUTH SWALLOWS
THE VIEWER.

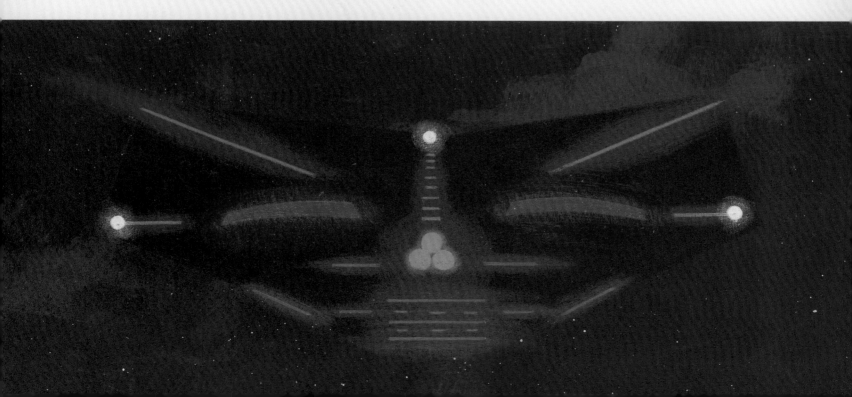

(Continued from page 152)

into." That included Spielberg. "I would come in at nine o'clock in the morning, and drill 'til about noon," he confirms.

As the Mothership started to take shape, Jein and his team included a number of items that one might not usually associate with a spaceship designed by a technologically superior species. "We just started putting all kinds of oddball stuff in there," he reveals. "World War II planes, a cemetery, a Volkswagen, a mailbox, and a shark. [Model builder] Dave Jones, who had just gotten off of *Star Wars*, put an R2-D2 there, and I said, 'Fine, we'll just leave it.'" When Trumbull saw it, he suggested they move the droid to the front of the ship and put a light on it. A *Star Wars* TIE fighter also made its way onto the model. "During the working process there was also a very heavy infusion of taco chips that got thrown in there," Jein recalls, laughing. "When the ship rotated you could kind of hear something swooshing around in there, and it smelled a little bit like peanut oil. It was a side effect of working long hours and eating at the same time."

It took eight and a half weeks to put the Mothership together, and when it was done, the model stood 38 inches tall, 63 inches in diameter, and weighed in at four hundred pounds. "It took four or five people to lift it onto its mount," says Jein.

With the Mothership complete, Jein and the crew moved on to the job of creating several more of the smaller UFOs that would be needed for a section of the Mothership finale referred to by the crew as the "barnstorming sequence," when even more UFOs arrive at Box Canyon to dazzle those in attendance.

"A lot of the saucers that were flying into Devils Tower were pretty strange-looking things as well," says Jein, whose team based the designs on a number of seemingly random objects. On one occasion, Spielberg dropped by carrying a Tonka truck, which he gave to Jein to make into a ship. "We did the Tonka truck, we did a toilet seat, we did a McDonald's sign, which we pulled because it was kind of obvious," Jein continues. "One of the guys did a gas mask. There's at least half a dozen of them, as well as the ones we used for the tollbooth scene, and the small red light that chases after them, dubbed the "Tinker light" [Spielberg's nod to the Disney version of the Peter Pan character Tinkerbell]. At one point we were just putting lights on anything just to get some more stuff in there."

PAGES 158–159 A wide array of everyday objects formed the basis for models of the smaller UFOs that accompany the Mothership.

PAGES 160–163 A wealth of colorful UFO concepts created by production illustrator George Jensen.

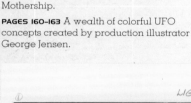

LIGHT SOURCE TO GLOW

McD? LOGO
SPINS TOWARD US

AS IT TURNS AND SLIPS
BY

③

SEEING THE UNDER-SIDE
AS IT ENTERS BOTTOM RIGHT

②

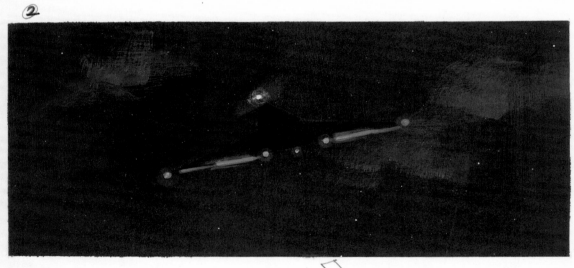

LEVELS OFF

①

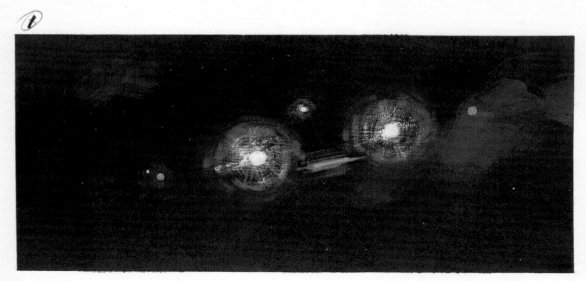

LANDING LIGHTS

COME ON —

1.

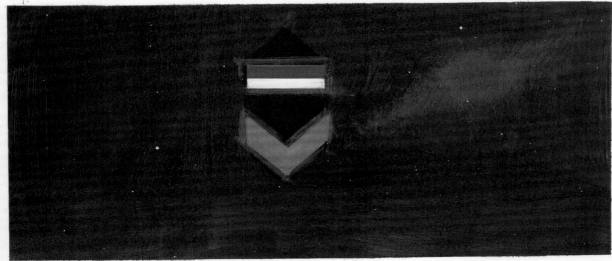

A BLACK SHAPE APPEARS
BEARLY VISIBLE
THE BANDS OF COLOR
POP ON CREATING THE
CHEVRON -

OTHER LIGHTS
COME ON -

2.

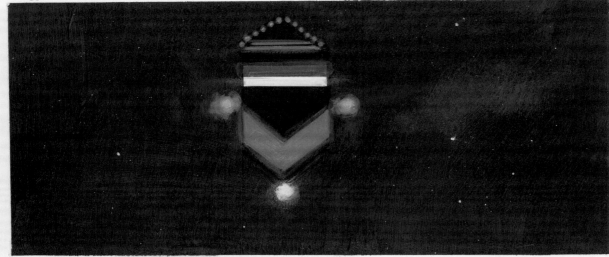

IT SLOWLY
RAISES ITS
NOSE AND
REVOLVES
PAST THE
CAMERA

3.

12

18

SMOKING REQUIRED

Once the Mothership and the other smaller spaceship models were fully assembled, it was time to shoot the visual effects film elements that would be expertly rephotographed into the live-action footage. Spielberg had decided that his UFOs would not have a hard-edged technological appearance, but rather would exude an ethereal quality. In all Hynek's reports of sightings, most witnesses remembered the bright lights of the ships, but not "the rivets," notes Trumbull. "Our intent was to create a soft, glowing, flared, and indistinct look," he explains. "I didn't want to do this hard-edged, object-type spacecraft against the black sky with stars, like we have already done in *2001*, and like *Star Wars* would become. I wanted *Close Encounters* to [have] diaphanous, beautiful, subtle, mystical, magical lighting."

OPPOSITE Camera test footage of the Mothership model.

ABOVE The console used to program the motion control camera.

BELOW The motion control camera between takes with the Mothership model visible in the background, positioned on its side for filming.

To that end, Trumbull created a "smoke room" in which the ships would be photographed. The interior of the room was blacked out, and special ventilation and laser smoke density measurement systems were created to circulate the smoke generated by a fogger machine. "The whole idea of the smoke room was to shoot miniatures in a very dense, almost impenetrable smoke environment in order to get beams of light and lens flares," Trumbull says.

Dave Stewart, who Richard Yuricich calls "the best motion control cameraman ever," ran the smoke room with his assistant David Hardberger. Trumbull and Yuricich first used the room to shoot the visual effects for the scene in which the UFO enthusiasts on Crescendo Summit mistake the lights of incoming military helicopters for alien visitors. With a large number of other UFO shots needing to be shot in the room, it was decided that the Mothership required its own dedicated space, and so a second smoke room was built down the block, at the annex of the Future General facility. The team also realized that the Mothership shoot was going to be so logistically difficult and time-consuming that it would need a dedicated visual effects cinematographer to oversee it. Dennis Muren, who had just finished work on *Star Wars*, was hired to take on the challenge.

Muren and Scott Squires helped to set up the Mothership smoke room, laying out various patterns of dolly tracks for the camera to move along and setting up the computer equipment

that would be used to control the camera's movement. Trumbull had been developing the computer control system, called the Mini-Scan (although it was the size of a refrigerator), since the early 1970s. The device could be programmed to control up to four pulse motors simultaneously, adjusting the camera's exposure and shutter speed, working a motor attached to the Mothership that would control the movement of the model, and driving a camera dolly that would move the camera along a predetermined path and at a set speed. The motor on the Mothership rig also allowed the model to spin as the camera moved toward and around it. Much mathematical calculation would be required to determine the length of each shot and the exact movements of the motorized Mothership model and the camera.

Muren and Squires would use the storyboards and notes from Spielberg and Trumbull as a guide for planning each segment to be filmed, lining up the shot, laying down tape at the beginning and end points for that individual piece of the sequence, and manually activating all the elements at the same time to carry out a test run. Digital LED counters would record the number of electric pulses required by each motor to create the desired action for the shot. When they were satisfied with the results, Muren and Squires would take these figures and input them into the Mini-Scan, which would then move the camera and model accordingly, filming the action.

The process itself was laborious and slow. The camera would move in tiny increments, sometimes as little as 1/100th of an inch per frame, and, depending on the shot and the level of exposure necessary, it could take hours to film a single segment.

Although the movement of the camera had been programmed precisely, it still needed to be monitored closely by Muren and Squires. If the extremely sensitive camera was impaired by a foreign object or bumped in any way, the shot could be ruined and have to be redone. They also needed to monitor the level of the smoke in the room every ten minutes to keep it as consistent as possible for continuity reasons. Since many of these shots could take longer than twelve hours at a time, Muren hired a UCLA student named Hoyt Yeatman to work the night shift to make sure that shooting continued uninterrupted.

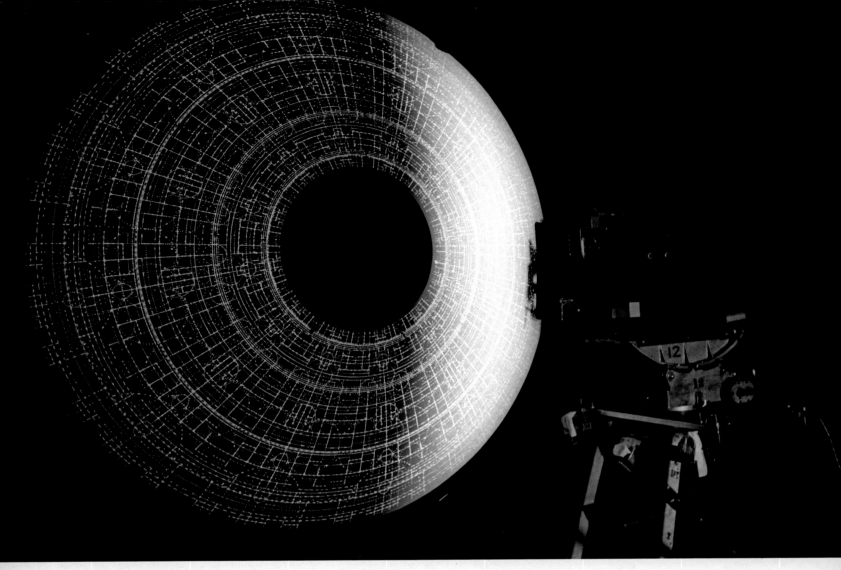

BRIGHT LIGHTS AND SHOOTING STARS

To make the dome on the underside of the Mothership sparkle with the brilliance of the San Fernando Valley at night, as per Spielberg's wishes, Douglas Trumbull turned to animation supervisor Robert Swarthe. To produce the effect, which would be most visible when the Mothership lands at Box Canyon, Swarthe created plates featuring a pattern resembling the grid-like lights that one might see from an airplane when flying over Los Angeles at night.

"It's difficult to make tiny points of light look really tiny on motion picture film, so we had to make the dots incredibly small," says Swarthe. To get the dots to be small enough, artist Harry Moreau created a single 30-degree pie-shaped section of tiny black dots on a 32-inch-long piece of white illustration board. This section gave Moreau the space he needed to make incredibly detailed patterns of dots. Then twelve duplicate copies of the finished wedge section were made and pasted together to form a full 360-degree circle four feet in diameter. That image was photographed onto 8-by-10-inch high-contrast negative film, which was projected onto the underbelly of the Mothership during the smoke room shoot. "Even after the Mothership photography had been completed, we often went back and added even more animation effects on the optical internegative," says Swarthe.

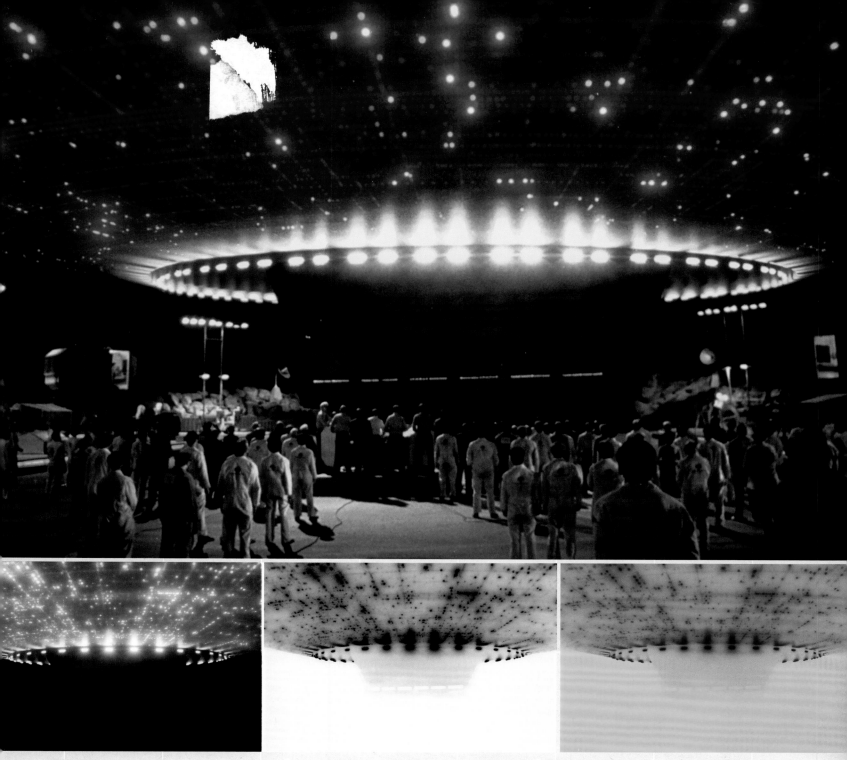

Swarthe was also responsible for creating the pattern of colored lights on the Mothership's underside that accompanies the aliens' response during their musical dialogue with the Project Mayflower team. The effect was shot using an Oxberry animation stand, with the camera shooting from above toward a flat platform (the "bed") with a very bright light shining up toward the camera. Swarthe employed a cardboard device (called a "slot gag") that contained small openings with color filters that were designed to match the areas on the live-action Mothership footage where lighting effects needed to be added. The slot gag was placed over the light on the stand and the slots

were opened and closed, the light shining through each colored filter in turn. Each individual colored light was shot one frame at a time, and the resulting images were later added to the negative.

"All the movements had to synchronize to the music, so I went over it all with [visual effects coordinator] Larry Robinson," says Swarthe. "We synced our effects to the five-tone musical soundtrack they used on the set when they photographed the live action."

In order to create starry sky elements for the film's many composite shots, Swarthe would use a technique that Trumbull had developed on *2001: A Space Odyssey*. He had Moreau take

OPPOSITE TOP The intricate pattern for the underbelly of the Mothership is projected onto the model as cameras record the effect.

OPPOSITE BOTTOM Artist Harry Moreau works on the design for the Mothership underbelly.

TOP A final frame from *Close Encounters* shows the dazzling lights on the underbelly of the Mothership.

ABOVE The hand-drawn patterns of lights for the underbelly of the Mothership were shot numerous times, using different combinations of filters and colors.

a sheet of Exeter paper, a black paper with a matte side that doesn't reflect light, and then use a low-pressure airbrush to sputter white paint on the paper in random patterns of tiny dots that looked like stars. "In some scenes we hand-painted the real constellation of Orion and eliminated some stars if there were too many," says Swarthe. The piece of Exeter paper itself would be placed on the animation stand, lit from above and photographed directly onto the undeveloped optical negative.

The stars were of particular importance to Spielberg, who would often remark to Swarthe that "the sky is the star of the picture!" Unfortunately, the tiny, detailed stars were also the element most susceptible to image degradation during the multiple rounds of duplication that the negative would endure in the process of adding each layer of special effects. To keep them at their sharpest, the star fields were the last element added to any visual effects shot.

Swarthe was also responsible for creating two other stellar *Close Encounters* moments: the scene where a number of UFOs assume a formation that mimics the Big Dipper over Devils Tower, and another where an apparent shooting star flies over the butte before splitting into four smaller lights, which then fly off. Both sequences were created using the animation stand.

"It was really kind of old-fashioned animation," says Swarthe. "We could hardly justify hundreds of thousands of dollars' worth of computer equipment and motion control motors for one or two shots, so we did it the more traditional way. After we finished with the animation, it was optically combined with the top of Devils Tower, which in this case was a retouched still photograph that we shot on the animation stand."

The exhaustive work of Swarthe and his team was just one aspect of creating a film that would ultimately boast more than two

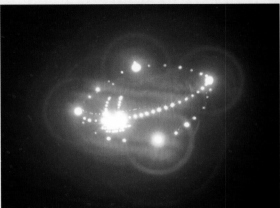

hundred separate visual effects, ranging from the breathtaking to those that are barely perceptible to most filmgoers. In today's era of sci-fi thrillers, it would take literally hundreds of technicians to accomplish the same thing that Trumbull did so brilliantly with a crew of just forty.

OPPOSITE Robert Swarthe and his team added thousands of stars to the negative of the film as the final step in the visual effects process.

LEFT A series of images shows the lights of the spaceships taking the form of the Big Dipper in the sky over Devils Tower as animated by Swarthe.

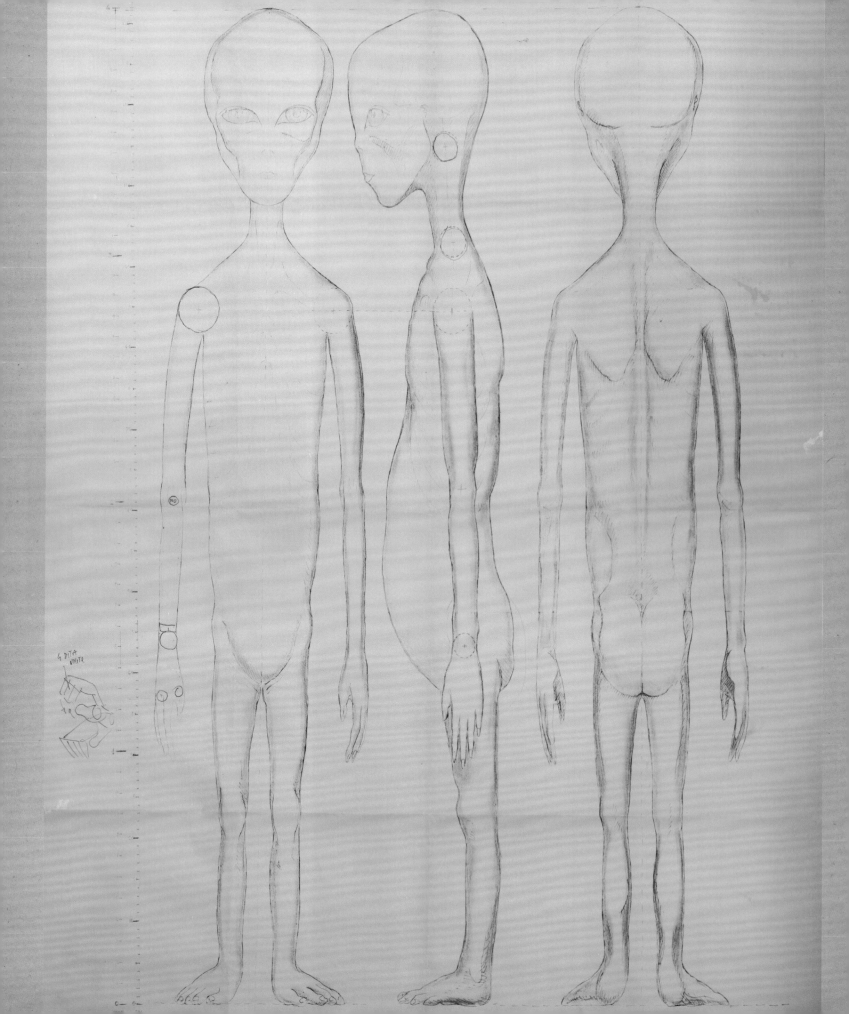

4 DITA
UNITE

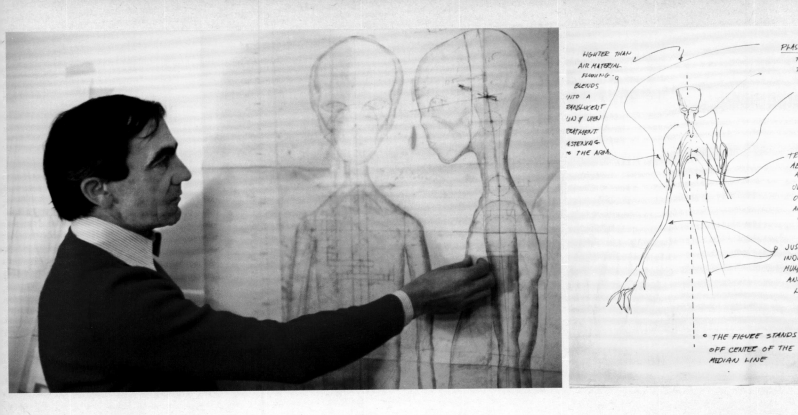

The figure stands off center of the median line

LIGHTER THAN AIR MATERIAL FLOWING BLENDS INTO A TRANSLUCENT UN & UEW TREATMENT & STERNING TO THE ARM

PLASTIC MATERIALS TRANSPARENT TRANSLUCENT

TRANSPARENT ABDOMINAL AREA - JUST A HINT OF THE RIBS AND ABDOMINAL CAVITY —

JUST A SLIGHT INDICATION OF HUMANOID ANATOMY IN THE LIMBS

ALTERED SPECIES

A few blocks away from Trumbull's visual effects facility, Spielberg and Kahn continued to assemble the film's footage into an initial rough cut. During the process, it became apparent to the director that, as he had feared, the aliens featured in close-ups were not working. In particular, the ET who returned Lacombe's hand signals was extremely unconvincing. Not only would Spielberg need to reshoot that scene with a newly designed alien, but he also wanted to improve the scene further by adding another ET: the first one to emerge from the ship. Both of these new aliens would purposely be designed to look different from the Grays, particularly the ET seen at the start of the sequence. "This completely different species would rise to full height and open its arms in a welcoming universal gesture," Spielberg says. "I wanted there to be diversity inside that particular civilization."

Spielberg turned to famed puppet master Bob Baker, known for his work on the *Star Trek* TV show and a variety of sci-fi films, including *The Angry Red Planet*, to create this first alien as a marionette. The design, featuring long, lanky, oversize arms and a semi-translucent body, would be heavily influenced by Spielberg's love of the work of Swiss painter and sculptor Alberto Giacometti.

For the alien who would exchange hand signals with Lacombe, Spielberg sought out acclaimed Italian special effects expert Carlo Rambaldi, who had just created the animatronic effects that would bring the title character in producer Dino De Laurentiis's *King Kong* (1976) to life (he would later win an Academy Award for his work on that film). The director asked Rambaldi if he could create an articulated alien puppet to use in the final scene, one that was

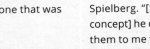

similar to the alien that Alves had originally designed based on the work of ufologist J. Allen Hynek, but with subtle differences. "Carlo created the fully operational mechanical alien we affectionately dubbed Puck," recalls Spielberg. "[Starting from Alves's original concept] he did numerous sketches and brought them to me to review, and together we agreed on the embryonic head, face, and thin neck that he sculpted in clay and then built. I needed the neck to be thin enough to convince an audience it wasn't just a kid in an alien mask and latex costume."

OPPOSITE AND ABOVE Carlo Rambaldi's sketches for the articulated alien puppet that came to be known as Puck.

TOP LEFT Carlo Rambaldi reviews the mechanics of his articulated Puck puppet.

TOP RIGHT Detailed design notes for puppeteer Bob Baker's marionette of the spindly alien that first alights from the Mothership.

CENTER RIGHT Puppeteer Bob Baker with the spindly alien marionette.

171

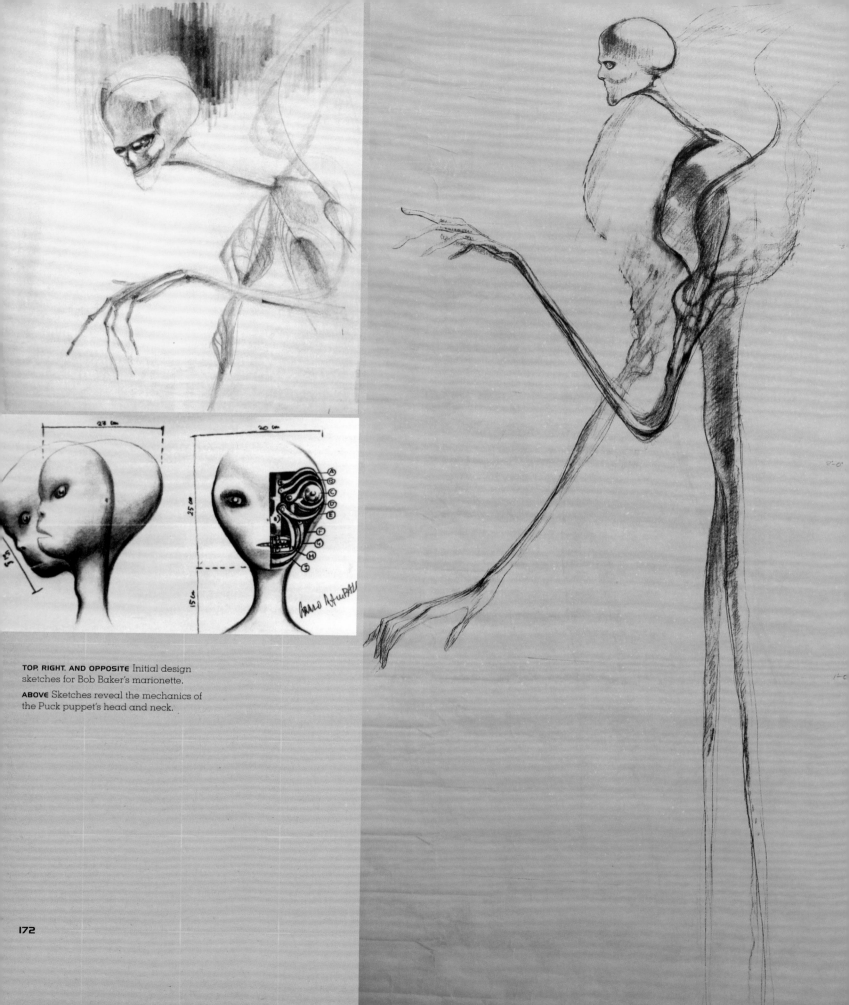

TOP, RIGHT, AND OPPOSITE Initial design sketches for Bob Baker's marionette.

ABOVE Sketches reveal the mechanics of the Puck puppet's head and neck.

172

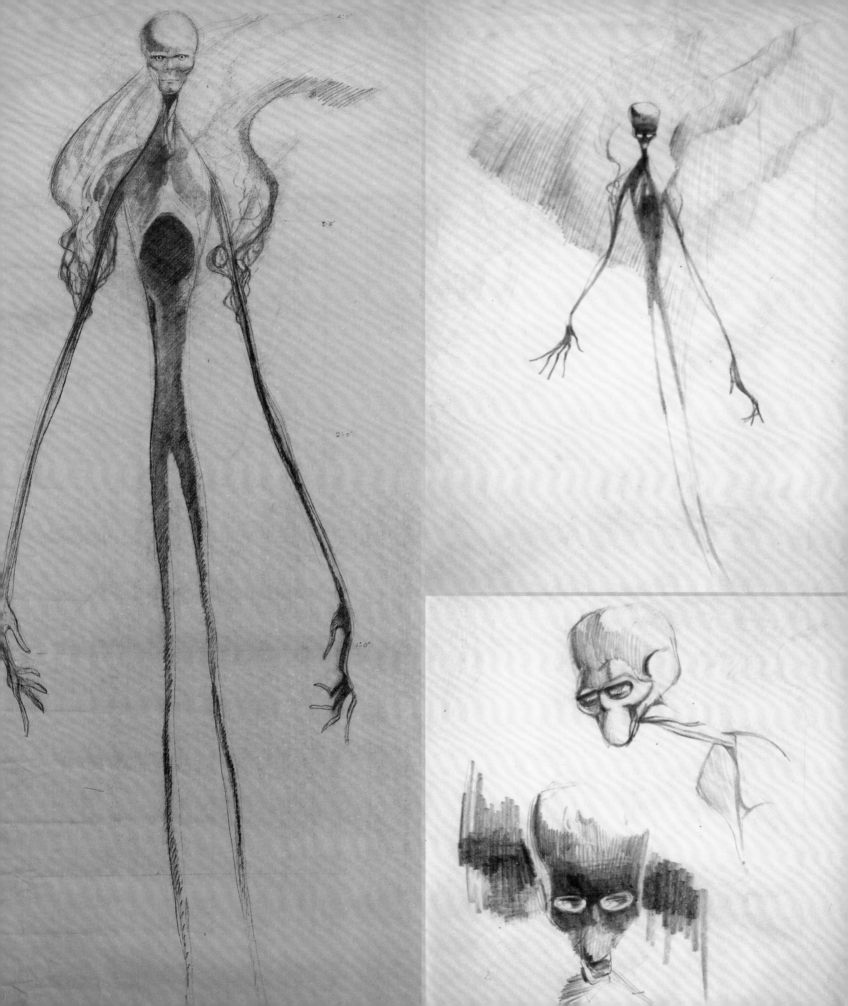

ONE MORE ROUND OF SHOOTING

Since it was already the end of February when Spielberg returned from India, and there was still much work to be completed in postproduction, the studio realized they would have to abandon the film's scheduled Easter 1977 release date. While Spielberg wanted the film to be released at Christmas, the studio promised exhibitors that *Close Encounters* would now premiere in mid-November.

TOP, ABOVE, AND OPPOSITE BOTTOM In California's Mojave Desert, Spielberg shoots the discovery of the missing WWII planes.

Shortly after the end of principal photography on *Close Encounters*, Stanley Jaffe had left Columbia Pictures to independently produce his own films, starting with *Kramer vs. Kramer*. Spielberg found a new ally in his replacement, Daniel Melnick. "Of all the studio heads, I got along best with Dan," says Spielberg. "He came in just as I was needing to shoot extra scenes. [I said,] 'I don't like my second cut. [There] are scenes I cut for budgetary reasons, three of which I need to put back, and there's other scenes I think the movie needs to make it more of an international story, not just a domestic one.' Dan agreed and gave us the extra money to go out and shoot more after we had long wrapped principal photography."

Shot on a fast-paced schedule between May 10 and 20, 1977, the extra scenes required Spielberg to call on a number of cinematographer friends to quickly step in and help. László Kovács (*Shampoo*), John A. Alonzo (*Chinatown*),

and William A. Fraker (*Rosemary's Baby*) all lent their talents to the production, and would be acknowledged in the final credits. Included in the extra scenes were the sequences featuring the new aliens that Bob Baker and Carlo Rambaldi had created. Since Baker's marionette would be seen emerging from the Mothership, a new hatch needed to be built for the shoot that would match the one used on the Big Set in Alabama. A scaled-down version was put together and the scenes shot in forced perspective to make the smaller set look as expansive as the one seen in the previously captured footage.

Another new scene had to be formulated when, during the editing process, Spielberg realized that there was no explanation for how Project Mayflower knew when and where the aliens would arrive on Earth. To fix the problem, he had Matthew Robbins and Hal Barwood write a scene where the Project Mayflower team review a set of seemingly random numbers that have been intercepted by their radio telescope. Laughlin subsequently identifies the mysterious numbers as the map coordinates for Devils Tower, revealing that before he was pressed into service as Lacombe's interpreter, he was a cartographer.

Melnick's approval of the additional shooting days also allowed Spielberg to film the excised opening from the original shooting draft, previously removed because it was deemed too expensive to realize. In the Mothership scenes filmed in Mobile, the abductee Navy pilots had been identified as being from Flight 19, but in all the footage captured up to this point there had been no exposition about the flight itself, nor was it mentioned in dialogue that the men had disappeared over the Bermuda Triangle. The new opening of the film would show Lacombe and his team discovering the pilots' decades-old planes, in mint condition in the middle of the desert. Spielberg had originally envisioned Lacombe finding the planes in the

middle of the Amazon jungle, but even with the additional funding from Columbia, shooting in a rainforest would not be financially feasible. Robbins and Barwood relocated the scene to the Sonoran Desert in Mexico, although it was actually shot in California's Mojave Desert. For the sake of story efficiency, they also chose to use this scene to introduce Lacombe to Laughlin,

replacing the two different versions of the limousine footage shot in Mobile.

To fill the scene with the requisite vintage aircraft, the production contacted a number of aeronautical enthusiasts who agreed to loan their planes for the duration of the shoot. For

ABOVE On Stage 29 at the Burbank Studios ranch facility, a pickup scene is shot to explain how the scientists know where the Mothership will land.

the actors, it proved to be another challenging sequence, as Spielberg had decided to set the action in the midst of a blinding sandstorm. Crew members threw large amounts of fuller's earth (a clay-based powder) in front of several huge fans, blasting the cast with a torrent of dust and making it extremely difficult for them to find their marks and be heard. Bob Balaban recalls one take where the strength of the wind generated by the powerful machines actually knocked him off his feet. He also recalls having to scream his lines over the roar, and being left to pick fuller's earth out of his beard for days after the scene was done.

Back in LA, Robbins and Barwood wrote one more scene for the film at the request of Spielberg. The sequence would revolve around the military men known as Team Leader and Wild Bill—played, respectively, by Merrill Connally and Warren Kemmerling—as they discuss executing the hoax that will result in the evacuation of the public from the area surrounding Devils Tower. Spielberg wanted to add the scene to make it clear that the military

forces in the film did not actually kill any of the animals with poison gas and instead were participating in a ruse.

The final day of shooting was dedicated to filming "Puck," the puppet that Carlo Rambaldi had constructed. A masterpiece of engineering, the creature stood four feet tall and was built with numerous mechanisms that would allow an operator to make the puppet's hand perform the Kodály signals necessary for the alien's big scene with Lacombe. The puppet's head was also articulated, and its face had been engineered to break into a smile, all actions operated through a system of cables. When designing the face, Rambaldi used pictures of Cary Guffey as inspiration, a resemblance that is clear in the final film when Puck smiles, an action operated on set by Spielberg himself. Although Puck was clearly attached to cables, when he was properly lit and the cameras started to roll, the character came to life, enthralling all who were present on set. It was a fitting way to end the filming of *Close Encounters of the Third Kind*.

PUBLIC ENCOUNTERS OF THE FIRST TIME

Spielberg continued to tinker with the film up until its release, his revisions partially informed by two test screenings Columbia Pictures held in Dallas in October of 1977, just a few weeks before its theatrical debut. The audience reaction at both screenings was overwhelmingly positive, but there was one audience member who didn't love anything about the movie. Despite all the secrecy and security surrounding the screenings, William Flanagan, a financial writer for *New York* magazine, had managed to sneak in, and soon published a scathing review, declaring that *Close Encounters* would be "a colossal flop." Because there had been so little public information about the film over the course of the shooting, Flanagan's review was picked up by countless other outlets, causing a panic among investors. Columbia's stock, which had started to regain solid footing based on positive buzz around the film, suddenly started to slide.

Fortunately, another writer, Frank Rich of *Time* magazine, had found a way into the same screening. His review was the polar opposite of Flanagan's, noting that the film was "richer and more ambitious than *Jaws*, and it reaches the viewer at a far more profound level than *Star Wars*." This piece, coupled with a press release from the studio condemning Flanagan's review and expressing confidence in the project, slowed the stock's decline.

"I didn't read either review," Spielberg says of the situation. "In those days, I was too terrified to read any reviews. I just let the news osmose into me."

While the director wasn't seeking out professional reviews, he was listening to the opinions of his audience. One particular area Spielberg was struggling with was the very end of the film and whether, during the closing

credits, he should use an original recording of "When You Wish Upon a Star" from Disney's *Pinocchio* (1940). Spielberg previewed the film to one test audience with the original recording of the song, sung by Cliff Edwards, and another without it. The audience response to the song itself was largely tepid, and those who didn't like it, recalls Spielberg, "were *adamant!*" In a 1978 interview for *Cinefantastique* magazine, he explained his final decision: "We felt the music, although it was a nice comment, seemed to have the effect to make a comment in reverse—that everything up until the last thirty minutes was a fantasy. Having seen the film both ways . . . it works better without the song."

Instead of using the Cliff Edwards recording itself, Spielberg ultimately opted for a more subtle way of weaving the melody into the fabric of his film. "Originally, we didn't include it in the

On November 16, 1977, *Close Encounters of the Third Kind* opened at the Ziegfeld Theater in New York and the famed Cinerama Dome in Hollywood, where it played to sold-out houses. One month later, the film expanded to 272 theaters across the country, and continued to do outstanding business until the end of its run in the summer of 1978. While Columbia had told Spielberg early on that they expected him to deliver a hit, the director surpassed their expectations and delivered a certified blockbuster, with a domestic gross totaling $116,395,460—the studio's highest-grossing film to date. The international release added another $171 million. Spielberg had single-handedly pulled the teetering studio from the brink of bankruptcy and turned its fortunes around.

At the 1978 Academy Awards ceremony, Vilmos Zsigmond received the Oscar for best cinematography for his work on the film, and Frank E. Warner received a Special Achievement Award for sound effects editing. Spielberg received a nomination as best director, and the film was nominated in six additional categories: Actress in a Supporting Role (Melinda Dillon), Art Direction, Film Editing, Music (Original Score), Sound, and Visual Effects. The Golden Globes nominated the film as Best Motion Picture—Drama and John Williams for his score, and Spielberg received nominations as both writer and director. Joe Alves was presented with a BAFTA award for his production design, and John Williams would take home a Grammy for his score, as well as a Grammy for the album of the film's music.

OPPOSITE TOP LEFT Audiences line around the block for the opening of *Close Encounters* at New York's Ziegfeld Theater.

OPPOSITE BOTTOM LEFT Spielberg reunites with François Truffaut at the royal premiere of the film in London.

ABOVE Producer Michael Phillips, Doug Trumbull with his wife, Ann Vidor, and Spielberg at the royal premiere.

BELOW Richard Dreyfuss, John Williams, Steven Spielberg, and Douglas Trumbull at the London premiere.

score," says composer John Williams. "While I was in Boston, conducting the Boston Pops, Steven asked me to write [music for] one of the ending scenes that included a strong reference to 'When You Wish Upon a Star.'" Recorded with the Boston Symphony Orchestra, the piece would include some very recognizable strains of the tune and play as the Mothership begins its ascent back into space. The theme would also be heard briefly earlier in the film, in the Neary house, from a Pinocchio music box sitting on Roy's model railroading tabletop.

THE SPECIAL EDITION

After *Close Encounters* finally hit theaters, Spielberg moved on to his next film, *1941*, a coproduction between Columbia Pictures and Universal Pictures. Although he was gratified with the critical and commercial success of *Close Encounters*, he could never shake the feeling that the final film didn't quite match his expansive vision for the story. Because of financial constraints and exhibitor obligations, he felt Columbia had forced him to release what he considered to be a "work print" of his movie.

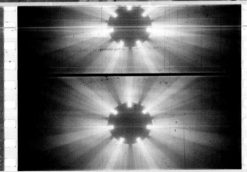

OPPOSITE AND TOP Production artist Ron Cobb's designs for the interior of the Mothership.

ABOVE One of the many visual effects created by Swarthe's animation team depicting the final burst of light from the "ballroom" ceiling of the Mothership interior.

"They had to get the film out," Spielberg acknowledges. "I just didn't feel it was the complete story I wanted to tell. There were other scenes I wanted to shoot that were in the script, and in the editing I discovered some scenes that I hadn't written which should have been in the script."

After *Close Encounters* finished its theatrical run in the summer of 1978, Spielberg asked Columbia if they would consider giving him the money to go back and finish the film the way he wanted, thereby offering them the chance to release a new, revised version of the movie in theaters. At the time, in the days before home video, it was standard practice, and very lucrative, to rerelease a popular film in theaters after its initial run. Spielberg's idea of updating the film was certainly attractive to the studio because it added a major selling point to the rerelease. However, their willingness to invest in revisiting the film would come with one major caveat. "They said,

'We're not going to reissue the film unless we are able to say in our advertising, "If you come to see *Close Encounters* again, we will show you something you've never seen before,"'" recalls Spielberg. "'We'll show you the inside of the Mothership.' That was the marketing decision I was faced with."

While Spielberg felt strongly that there were elements of the original version that he wanted to tweak and expand upon, he was torn over having to put on the screen a piece of the story he had always thought belonged to the imagination of the audience. Ultimately, the lure of getting to fix his film won out. "I wanted to finish what I felt I had only partially completed," he states. "I felt it was worth selling out to be able to have that opportunity to show the film again."

Columbia gave Spielberg $2 million for the reshoots, but the director wouldn't be able to give his complete attention to the Special Edition until he had first completed filming *1941*,

183

TOP AND CENTER LEFT Almost two and a half years after wrapping the original film, Richard Dreyfuss returned to shoot Roy Neary's entrance into the Mothership. The shot showing the aliens lining up to greet Neary would not make the final cut.

OPPOSITE Ron Cobb's design for the wall seen in the interior of the Mothership. Hundreds of aliens can be seen observing Neary's arrival.

ABOVE Greg Jein and crew built a miniature fifteen-foot version of Cobb's wall, complete with hundreds of half-inch plastic aliens.

which began shooting in October 1978 and would wrap in late May of 1979. In the meantime, he reassembled his team in preparation. After *Close Encounters*, Douglas Trumbull and Richard Yuricich had been hired by Paramount Pictures to fix the effects on *Star Trek: The Motion Picture*, a pressure-filled assignment that proved to be extremely grueling. As a result, Trumbull passed on the chance to be involved with the Special Edition. Meanwhile, Richard Yuricich agreed to participate in the early stages of planning the visual effects for the new scenes, on the understanding that he would then step away for a very necessary vacation. Both he and Trumbull recommended that Spielberg hire animator Robert Swarthe to oversee the visual effects, with Dave Stewart supervising the effects photography. Spielberg agreed and also brought back Greg Jein, who had been working on *1941*, and would lead the model-making team for the Special Edition.

Ron Cobb, who had worked as a concept artist on *Star Wars* and *Alien*, was brought in to design the interior of the Mothership, and to create the storyboards for the new sequence. Cobb used the exterior of the Mothership as his starting point and came back with several designs that carried its general aesthetic to the interior, thereby creating a unified look between the inside and outside of the ship. The centerpiece of his proposed designs was a grand space in which the smaller UFOs would fly back and forth and dock. Like the exterior of the ship, the docking area was adorned with thousands of twinkling lights.

The scene itself would pick up from the moment that Roy Neary walked up the ramp and disappeared into the ship in the original film. In the Special Edition, after being met by the aliens at the top of the ramp, he would walk down a corridor, and next be seen entering an enclosed and somewhat unspectacular circular chamber (known to the crew as "the Roundhouse"), the ceiling of which suddenly begins to levitate upward, revealing the full resplendence of the docking area that Ron Cobb had designed. (The crew nicknamed this area "the Ballroom.") One full-size partial set would be constructed for the ramp and interior of the hatch, but the rest of the Mothership interiors would be created using miniatures and other visual effects. Work on the miniature sets began in the summer of 1979.

While Spielberg hadn't intended to shoot any of the live action until he was totally through with *1941*, Richard Dreyfuss's schedule was so busy that he could spare only one day in February 1979 for the Special Edition shoot. As

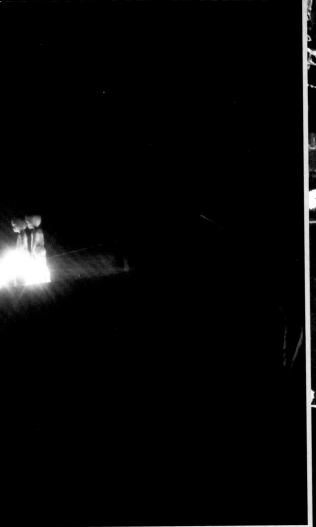

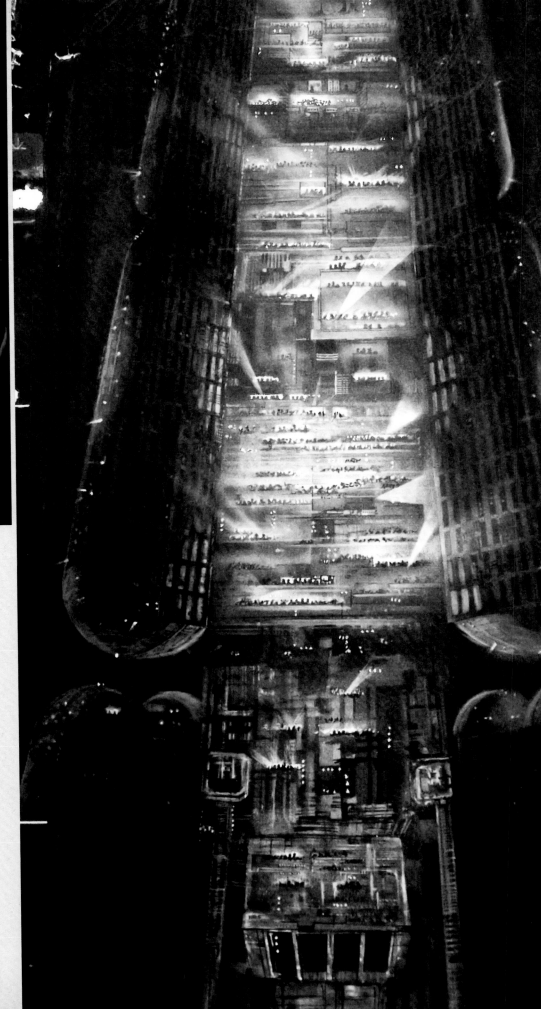

a result, the director had to film the footage that required Dreyfuss nearly a whole year before he started directing the rest of the Special Edition scenes. Once again donning his red jumpsuit, almost two and a half years after he had ascended the ramp back in Mobile, Dreyfuss was filmed walking up a newly constructed version of the ramp, this time moving toward the camera before stopping to take in his new surroundings. Spielberg had also cast a number of young girls to play Grays and had the little aliens line both walls of the hatch interior to welcome Neary into their ship. The director would later discard that footage, however, feeling that the moment should focus solely on Neary.

Knowing that the ETs would need to be glimpsed somewhere within the Mothership, Spielberg had Greg Jein build a 15-by-12-foot model of a large wall from the Ballroom location that featured hundreds of viewing ports, each crowded with aliens trying to get a look at their new visitor. The wall was constructed with materials cribbed from the already filmed Mothership interior sets, and the balconies were filled with several hundred half-inch plastic aliens. All would be visible only as tiny silhouettes, wreathed in smoke to further obscure their appearance. For long shots on the miniature sets that needed to

Carolina, to Havana, Cuba. An old 29-foot-long model of a ship had been located on the back lot at Twentieth Century Fox, and Jein took several days to refurbish it. He had previously unearthed a photograph of the real *Cotopaxi*, and while his model bore precious little resemblance to the original, Jein and Spielberg agreed they should move ahead with it regardless, as most audience members wouldn't know the difference.

In late January 1980, François Truffaut was unavailable to reprise his role as Lacombe, so Spielberg asked Bob Balaban and J. Patrick McNamara (who appeared onscreen in the newly released *1941*) to return and anchor the scene. "I thought it was great that Steven had a chance, as all filmmakers would like to, to slightly refine something that was already pretty wonderful to begin with," says Balaban.

Although set in the Gobi Desert, the scene was filmed near Death Valley, California, where the location was peppered with helicopters, jeeps, dozens of extras, and camels. Rather than rely on special photographic equipment or postproduction effects, Spielberg shot the scene of Laughlin and company examining the ship using forced perspective. With the model of the *Cotopaxi* placed prominently in the foreground, lying against a dune, all the other elements, including the actors and vehicles, were actually about

ABOVE AND BELOW Greg Jein's *Cotopaxi* model is filmed in Death Valley, California.

OPPOSITE Spielberg once again directs his gang of Grays.

feature Roy Neary, Jein sculpted Dreyfuss's face onto a 6-inch radio-controlled action figure that would pass for the actor when used as a very small part of the frame.

Spielberg began work in earnest in January of 1980, several weeks after the theatrical release of *1941*. His first scene was one he had been forced to drop for budgetary reasons—the discovery by Lacombe and company of the SS *Marine Sulphur Queen*. He would finally be able to have his ship, but would decide to change its identity to the SS *Cotopaxi*, a cargo ship that had vanished in 1925, en route from Charleston, South

two hundred yards away, in the background, performing their actions as if the full-size ship were directly in front of them. "It really did appear as though there was a giant ship and we were little people wondering why it was there," says Balaban. "Once again, we looked at something that wasn't there, and I think I got quite used to it. My ability to look at things that aren't there has greatly improved since that movie."

With the Special Edition footage completed, Spielberg and Michael Kahn began re-editing the film. They started by removing a number of scenes that Spielberg had come to regard as unnecessary, most notably the sequence where Roy trashes the neighborhood to collect materials for building his Devils Tower replica. The Air Force press conference scene was also removed, as was a scene from the beginning of the film showing Roy at the power company's HQ, and Carl Weathers' scene during the town evacuation sequence. The scene of Roy breaking down in the shower that had been shot for the original film but not used was included, giving Ronnie Neary more motivation for leaving her husband. Little snippets of dialogue were removed here and there, and when Spielberg was done, the running time of

the Special Edition was three minutes shorter than the original.

Close Encounters of the Third Kind: Special Edition opened on August 1, 1980, in North America, with the international release following shortly after. The film grossed a respectable $16 million, with Columbia again profiting greatly from its investment. The critical reception was mixed, with some reviewers agreeing that the changes made for a more focused, emotional, and cohesive film, while others felt there was no need for Spielberg to have tampered with what they considered a masterpiece. In particular, the consensus among critics and the general public was that adding the interior of the Mothership had not enhanced the experience.

"Looking back on it, based on who I am now, I wish I had never made that deal and wish I had never exposed the inside of the Mothership," Spielberg says.

In 1997, the director had the opportunity to go back one last time to create his third version of the film, which was released the following year on DVD as "The Collector's Edition." The very first thing he did was to excise every frame of the interior of the Mothership.

WHEN YOU WISH UPON A STAR

Forty years after it first premiered in theaters, *Close Encounters of the Third Kind* continues to linger in the imaginations of audiences the world over. While its success can be measured in stellar box office returns and critical accolades, its real triumph is the creation of a new visual lexicon for those pondering the greatest mystery of our existence: Are we alone in the universe?

Spielberg's film was the first to take the prospect of alien visitation seriously, and depicted first contact between ETs and mankind in such vivid and imaginative detail that four decades after the film's release it's almost impossible to think of UFOs and not see some aspect of *Close Encounters* in the mind's eye.

The film has been absorbed into our culture in such an absolute way that the slightest allusion to its iconic visuals and soundtrack evokes an instant association to not only *Close Encounters* but to all aspects of ufology. As a result, the film has been referenced and parodied countless times throughout the years, from a nod to the Five Notes in the James Bond adventure *Moonraker*, released just two years after *Close Encounters*, to affectionate spoofs in pop-culture-savvy TV shows including *The Simpsons*, *Saturday Night Live*, and *South Park*.

The film's influence has also been officially recognized by a variety of prestigious institutions. In the United States, *Close Encounters* was inducted into the National Film Registry in 2007, recognized as "culturally, historically, or aesthetically significant" and earmarked for preservation by the Library of Congress. Additionally, the American Film Institute included the feature on its list of the 100 Greatest American Movies of All Time.

For those who created the film, their appreciation of *Close Encounters* is much more personal, the experience a high point of their storied careers.

"It was the first motion picture that I wrote and directed," says Spielberg. "It's something I had dreamed about as a child. Then I grew into a movie director, and had the opportunity to make my childhood dreams come true."

"What a profoundly important story to tell," adds Richard Dreyfuss. "I've always maintained that mankind shows its maturity by asking the most extraordinary questions, and shows its immaturity by answering. We're not old enough to answer these questions, but goddamn, I'm impressed with us that we ask them. Participating in *Close Encounters* was my way of being a part of the question."

Hosting a New York screening of *Close Encounters* in 2017, Bob Balaban got to once again witness the awesome emotional power of the film, the reaction reminding him of when he first watched the film with an audience back in 1977.

"People were pulling out their handkerchiefs and weeping at the beauty of the end of the movie," says the actor. "I think the legacy of *Close Encounters* is that it's a real example of how Steven can have such an amazing ability to create illusions in movies that are enormous and involve a tremendous amount of technique, people, machinery, and yet is still able to make a movie that's tremendously personal and very emotional."

While *Close Encounters of the Third Kind* may have left an indelible impression on the imaginations of audiences everywhere, whenever Spielberg himself thinks of the film, the first image that springs to his mind is from the abduction sequence: As Barry Guiler opens the front door to welcome the visitors, the room is filled with a golden hue, the little boy bathed in, and silhouetted by, the light. "It's what all of us do, when we open any door to a new idea," he reflects. "And any new idea, really, is like a blast of light—especially if it catches us and takes hold and we do something about it, and we make something out of it. So to me it was symbolic of everything I've ever done in making movies."

TOP Spielberg and Dreyfuss confer on the set.

BELOW Spielberg and Truffaut on the Box Canyon set.

OPPOSITE Production art perfectly captures the iconic visuals of *Close Encounters of the Third Kind*.

ACKNOWLEDGMENTS

In October 1977, as a college film critic in New York, I was thrilled to get an invitation from the Columbia Pictures publicity department to be a part of a press junket for their upcoming release of *Close Encounters of the Third Kind*. I would be flown to Los Angeles, attend a screening of the film, and have the chance to interview the cast and filmmakers. One week later, I received another letter informing me that due to unforeseen circumstances, the junket had been canceled.

As consolation, I was invited to the premiere of the film in New York, where I sat spellbound watching what I considered a masterpiece of filmmaking and storytelling. I still do.

Forty years later, I found out why the press event in LA was called off. Steven Spielberg was still editing the film and would continue to do so up until about two weeks before it arrived in theaters. While I wasn't able to interview anybody back in the day, I hit the jackpot in the writing of this book. It was worth the wait.

Quite simply, this book wouldn't have been possible without Steven Spielberg. Not only did he make himself available to me, granting his invaluable time and recollections, but he also readily opened his private archives to share materials that enhanced and elevated this work to another level.

The cast was equally as giving in sharing their time, memories, and insights. Sincere thanks to Richard Dreyfuss, Melinda Dillon, Bob Balaban (whose amazing *Close Encounters Diary*, written back in 1977, was an invaluable aid), Cary Guffey, and Carl Weathers.

As Steven Spielberg has stated time and time again, *Close Encounters* would not be the film it is without the involvement of the extraordinary talent behind the camera. I feel the same way about their contributions to this book. Thanks to Michael Phillips, Joe Alves, Roy Arbogast, Peter Anderson, Hal Barwood, Jim Bloom, Rocco Gioffre, David Hardberger, Susan Heldfond, Stanley Jaffe, Gregory Jein, Michael Kahn, Dennis Muren, Kevin Pike, Steven Poster, Matthew Robbins, Scott Squires, Robert Swarthe, Juliet Taylor, Douglas Trumbull, John Williams, and Richard Yuricich.

At Amblin Partners, Michelle Fandetti and Marvin Levy went above and beyond in their efforts on my behalf, and I can't thank them enough for their help. Thanks to Lauren Elliott, Brittani Lindman, and Kristin Stark as well.

I have been truly fortunate to have the support and guidance of Chris Prince, Jon Glick, Vanessa Lopez, and Robbie Schmidt from Insight Editions. I thank you all.

Thanks to Virginia King at Sony Pictures and to Gilbert Emralino at the Sony archives.

Thanks also to the Margaret Herrick Library, Academy of Motion Picture Arts and Sciences, for providing important materials from their collection.

No less important are the contributions and support of the following, to whom I express my thanks: Jocelyn Andrews, Bradley Cherna, Bob Gale, Mindy Johnson, Rita Klastorin, Gene Kozicki, Justin Lubin, Michael Matessino, Daniel Noah, Steven and Virginia Reeser, Lucas Seastrom, Michael Singer, Hopper Stone, Josh C. Waller, Lisa Whalen, and Elijah Wood.

For Ardemis and Minnie . . .

—Michael Klastorin, 2017

**CLOSE ENCOUNTERS OF THE THIRD KIND:
THE ULTIMATE VISUAL HISTORY**

Published by Titan Books, London, in 2017.

**TITAN
BOOKS**

*A division of Titan Publishing Group Ltd
144 Southwark Street
London SE1 0UP
www.titanbooks.com*

 Find us on Facebook: www.facebook.com/titanbooks

Follow us on Twitter: @Titanbooks

Published by arrangement with Insight Editions, PO Box 3088, San Rafael, CA 94912, USA.
www.insighteditions.com

A CIP catalogue record for this title is available from the British Library.

ISBN: 9781785657283

PUBLISHER: Raoul Goff

ASSOCIATE PUBLISHER: Vanessa Lopez

ART DIRECTOR: Chrissy Kwasnik

DESIGNER: Jon Glick

SENIOR EDITOR: Chris Prince

MANAGING EDITOR: Alan Kaplan

EDITORIAL ASSISTANT: Hilary VandenBroek

PRODUCTION EDITOR: Rachel Anderson

PRODUCTION MANAGERS: Alix Nicholaeff and Lina s Palma

PRODUCTION ASSISTANT: Jacob Frink

Insight Editions, in association with Roots of Peace, will plant two trees for each tree used in
the manufacturing of this book. Roots of Peace is an internationally renowned humanitarian
organization dedicated to eradicating land mines worldwide and converting war-torn lands
into productive farms and wildlife habitats. Roots of Peace will plant two million fruit and
nut trees in Afghanistan and provide farmers there with the skills and support necessary for
sustainable land use.

Manufactured in China

10 9 8 7 6 5 4 3 2 1